Walk Awhile in My Autism

A manual of sensitivity presentations
to promote understanding of people on the autism spectrum

Kate McGinnity
Nan Negri

Illustrations by Ben Averill

Cambridge Book Review Press
2005

Cambridge Book Review Press
310 North Street
Cambridge, Wisconsin 53523
Editor: Bob Wake

Cover design by Tom Pomplun

ISBN 0-9660376-4-2

Library of Congress Control Number: 2004115586

Walk Awhile in My Autism
can be ordered online at www.walkawhile.org

To my great nephew, Max.
I hope this book will contribute in some small way
to you growing up in a world where you are accepted
and understood as deeply as you are already loved.
And to my son, August,
who holds the entire universe in his agate eyes.
—K. M.

To Matt, Nathan, Liz, Carissa, David and Grady ...
children I have loved, then peers to one another, then friends ...
you showed me how it happens.
And to Dad ...
you always knew I could ... and I always will.
—N. N.

CONTENTS

PREFACE

It was a cool, crisp sunny day in early autumn. The elementary playground was filled with bubbling children. I walked out in search of my own students. All of them were on the autism spectrum and were supported by a variety of adults. I did a quick head count, locating all but one of them among the other students. At closer look, I found him, crouched in the middle of the sandbox, covering his eyes and crying silently as a circle of general education students threw sand at him, getting it in his eyes, nose, mouth and all over his body.

I rescued John, checked my anger and brought the other students back inside the school to conference with them about their misbehavior. The first question I asked them was, "What brought you to do something so mean?"

These were not bad kids. I knew several of them and they were high achievers, athletes, popular ... They responded that they didn't understand why John didn't run or leave or fight back, and they just got caught up in watching his lack of response.

This is a true story of the type of occurrence that is all too common in our schools. Stories and experiences like these moved us to write this book.

Kate McGinnity
Nan Negri
August, 2004

INTRODUCTION

Fear is the enemy of intimacy. Education can be the antidote to that fear. It is our hope that through the materials and activities set out in this book, we can help create a more open and accepting environment for all children, including students with autism.* If we truly want children with autism to be understood and accepted, we have an obligation to teach their peers how to have successful relationships with them. This requires providing classmates accurate information about how individuals with autism perceive and experience the world. The benefits of this type of teaching far surpass facilitating the individual relationship a "typical" child may have with one who has autism. Since these peers will be the future teachers, bosses, neighbors, parents and family members of individuals with autism, the compassion, understanding and accommodation skills they learn will have lifelong positive effects.

Regardless of the age and level of challenge experienced by an individual with autism or the structure of service delivery, there will undoubtedly be a need to teach the people surrounding that person about who he or she is. These people can use the teachings to be appropriately responsive to the educational, emotional, social, communication, and spiritual needs presented by someone with autism.

Our goal is to provide a menu of teachings to help others learn about the unique ways in which individuals with autism experience this world. We have attempted to provide teachings that match a variety of learning styles and are appropriate for all ages of students. While these sensitivity strategies have been primarily devel-

---

* In this book, the term "autism" will be used in the educational sense, referring to individuals who fall anywhere on what Lorna Wing characterizes as the "Autism Continuum" and is currently referred to as "Autism Spectrum Disorders."

oped for school settings, they have applicability in a variety of non-school settings as well, including vocational sites, adult living facilities, day care settings, neighborhood and community settings, and family groups. Additionally, while our focus has been specifically on students with autism, there is obviously application across all areas of challenge and difference.

Our greatest learnings on this topic have come directly from individuals who themselves experience autism. Chapter One, "Speaking for Themselves," begins by offering strategies in which individuals with autism "speak" for themselves. We describe and discuss a variety of ways a person with autism can provide information to their peers, either directly or indirectly. Through listening to our friends and acquaintances who have autism, we have learned how vital true intimacy is to their lives. Increasing peer awareness is a necessary step toward dissipating the fear that so often serves as an obstacle to relationship development.

In Chapter Two, "Sensitizing Peers," we provide a series of activities which allow the peers of individuals on the autism spectrum to experience various aspects of autism. There are many styles of learning, but for most of us direct experience is the supreme learning tool. We've taken information that we've gathered from people with autism, their families, teachers and others who care about them and developed activities that are designed to literally allow us to "walk awhile in their autism." The activities begin with a visualization exercise that encourages peers to experience the "whole" of autism, including how the senses impact social and communication interactions. Visualization can be effective for many learners. Others may require more active participation to experience another's perspective. The activities that follow the visualization involve more active participation and address the following aspects of the experience of autism:

• Appreciating diversity and differing preferences.

• Different cognitive styles.

• Experiencing movement differences.

- Sensory differences.

- Neurological differences, including messages and the brain.

- Monochannel functioning.

- Exclusion and social barriers.

- Social and communication differences and challenges.

- Cycle of helping, receiving too much or too little.

For each activity, the reader is provided a description of the overall activity, directions on how to set it up, a list of the materials that will be needed, and suggested points to make following the activity.

In Chapter Three, "Pulling It All Together," we address individualizing and choosing the activities which best fit your situation. Information based on peer surveys/questions can be utilized for this purpose. These surveys/questions are discussed and specific examples are given. One high school speech/language therapist, for instance, combined and individualized some of the activities for a broader sensitivity training, which she made available to all the students in her high school setting. As staff and family members, we are sometimes called upon to provide sensitivity or awareness training to different groups in our communities. In doing this, we broaden the umbrella of understanding and create a wider circle of emotional safety and increased tolerance for individuals with autism. Chapter Three offers suggestions and guidance for sensitivity training outside of the school environment. Awareness materials are included in the Appendix for putting together an effective presentation.

A final chapter, "The Magic of Relationship," presents what we consider some of the tangible results of successful sensitivity training. Through the use of essays, journal entries and stories written by siblings and peers of individuals with autism, we celebrate the blossoming of compassion.

1. SPEAKING FOR THEMSELVES

*Individuals with autism providing information
about themselves to their peers*

One of the most powerful encounters for a classmate or co-worker can be to listen to someone with autism speak about their experience of the world. Of course, for many people with autism, even very verbal people with autism, talking about themselves can be difficult or impossible. Fortunately, a wonderful group of individuals with autism from Britain and the United States have put together a short videotape that "speaks" for those who can't. Titled *A is for Autism* (see Appendix, page 143), the film uses their own words and visual images to demonstrate how they see, feel and hear. They talk about the unpredictability of their experiences given the ever changing way in which their sensory systems work. They talk about how they "crave tender touch, but then feel overwhelmed by it like a tidal wave." They share the kinds of things that are important to them: numbers, trains, routines, and peers' perceptions of them. The video, which lasts only 11 minutes, provides a powerful springboard for a discussion about the moment by moment challenges faced by someone with autism. Its use in presentations can facilitate discussions that address at least some of the following issues:

- What it's like to have a sensory system that operates upredictably and inconsistently.

- What it's like to have words you want to speak, but can't.

- What it's like to hear words, sometimes catching their meaning and sometimes not.

• What it's like when words feel like bullets in your ears.

• What it's like when emotion makes it hard to pay attention.

• What it's like to feel spaces shrink on you.

• What it's like to use one kind of sensory stimulation to block out another.

A classroom viewing of *A is for Autism* can be used as a prompt for discussion purposes or as an introduction for a series of sensitivity activities.

Following are some additional examples of individuals with autism speaking for themselves. They use a variety of approaches, including writing/illustrating books, giving speeches, displaying photographs, and sharing artwork. Some individuals prefer to present information specific to themselves, while others share about autism in general. Sharings may be created and presented independently or with various levels of assistance.

A Book Written for a Class

One student who is nonverbal had anxiety about entering second grade, since some of his peers would be different than in the first grade. He was encouraged to write a book about himself telling his friends what he wanted them to know about him. Because direct interaction was difficult for him, the book was just left out on the counter with other library books and the other children were discreetly informed of its presence. This young person was able to share information about himself with his peers without direct interaction. Using this strategy honored his individual style and allowed his peers to obtain a deeper understanding of his experience of autism.

Another student, Dylan, is in upper elementary school. As part of transitioning to the next grade level, his sister helped him write a book about himself. They combined the narrative with photographs to provide peers with a sense of who Dylan is.

Here is his story:

I Am Me

Everybody is different. We look different, dress different, talk different. We eat what we like and listen to music we like. Some kids wear their hair long or shave it all off; mine's short. I have brown eyes. Yours might be blue or green. I am tall and skinny. You might be short or somewhere in-between. These are the things that make you who you are.

All of us like to do different things. Some of us like to play football; I like basketball. You might like to play N64 or Gamecube; I like to play Playstation. You might like to skateboard or ride bikes, go to the movies or watch TV. Me, I like to do all of these. I also like boating and swimming and teasing my sister, too.

We all have families and friends, who each has their own way of living. Some of us are good at sports; some of us are not. But we are all good at something that someone else is not. I do things my way and you do things yours. Learning to understand each other helps us to care a little more. One of the things that makes me "me" is that I have a learning disorder called autism.

It's a problem with my senses that makes me feel nervous all the time. Loud noises and large crowds hurt my ears and make me uncomfortable. Smelly smells make me dizzy and bright lights hurt my eyes. When everything is thrown at me all at one time, it sends my head spinning and makes me all uptight. So, sometimes I talk movie talk to help me feel all right. I may act a little strange, but I will soon be all right.

If you want to help me out and be a good friend, ask me to slow down and use my words instead. Point me in the right direction and help me follow the rules. Help me with my school work and on the playground. I'll repay you with my friendship and accept you for you. If we can all accept we're different in our own way, there'd be a lot less problems in this world today. I am Dylan and I am me. I am different from you and you're different from me.

A Speech Written and Presented to a Class

When Mark was in late elementary school, the class did a project about various differences in people. He decided to teach his classmates about himself and his autism through a short autobiographical speech. Even though he was verbal, it was difficult for him to readily access his language, especially when he was nervous. Therefore, his special education support staff assisted him first in writing his speech and then putting it on 3x5 cards. Reading aloud from the cards, he presented the speech, which was received with an overwhelmingly positive attitude by his peers:

Hi, I'm Mark Matthews.
I want to talk about me because I have autism.
First I will tell you about me.
I am mostly the same as other kids like you.
I like to play major league baseball and either Nintendo or computer games.
I also like to play basketball outside.
I went to see *Men in Black* at the movie theatre.
I like to watch TV. I like to watch baseball games.
I went horseback riding at Three Gates this summer.
My horse is named Missy.
I like to go to Culver's to eat.
I have the best dinner.
I have large french fries and drink Pepsi at Culver's.
Because I have autism, I am also different from other kids.
It's harder for me to just talk to people.
Some noises hurt my ears.
Some noises work just fine with me.
The headphones help me. It makes things quieter.
It feels different to have autism.
I have different words in my head that make it hard to listen to other words.
Sometimes on Thursday I go to Culver's to eat lunch.
Friends go with me.
KIDS, WOULD YOU LIKE TO GO TO CULVER'S WITH ME?

A Speech and Art Display for a Wider Audience

Matthew Ward is an individual with high-functioning autism who is currently a senior at the UW-Madison majoring in mathematics. He is living by himself in his own apartment with minimal support from his family and broker (caseworker). Matt provides a wonderful gift to our field through his willingness to share information about his life experience with us. He often brings examples of his origami and other artwork to share. Here is an early version of a speech he presented to a state-wide training on educating adolescents with autism, which was followed by a question and answer period:

My name is Matt Ward. I am 20 years old. I live in Cottage Grove, Wisconsin (a suburb of Madison) with my mom and stepfather (Nancy and Tom Alar) and my little sister, Elizabeth. I am a special student at Monona Grove High School, the University of Wisconsin, and the Madison Area Technical College (MATC). I am also taking my third semester of honors calculus courses at the University of Wisconsin.

My parents found out I was autistic when I was 18 months old. I said my first word and learned my name when I was two. I had a really hard time learning to talk. I knew only 30 words when I was three. Half of those words were the names of numbers. I started using short sentences when I was four. Sometimes I would repeat things that I heard from other people or on the TV. I asked my first question when I was five. For a long time I mixed up my pronouns. I would say things like "You want a cookie," when I meant I wanted a cookie.

My favorite toy when I was two was a jar lid. I loved to spin them. I used to try to spin everything. I could even spin Kleenex boxes. I was in a very structured day care center from the time I was three months old until I was two. My family thinks that this led to an early diagnosis. From ages 2-5, I was in the Waisman Center Day Care Center at the University of Wisconsin. Only a few of the kids there were disabled.

In grade school I spent about half of the time in an ED-LD classroom and half the time with regular students. I usually had an aid with me, especially in the regular classes.

The transition to junior high was stressful because I had to go to a different room for each class, but I managed it. I went to almost all regular classes in junior high and still usually had an aid with me. When things got rough, I went to a resource room.

Some autistic people are also retarded, but I am not. A lot of the kids in my classes thought I was retarded because I looked and acted kind of weird. I got picked on a lot in junior high because I was so different. I didn't know the social rules and sometimes did strange things or made strange noises. For example, I really liked Bugs Bunny and Road Runner cartoons when I was younger. I can call up memories of things like cartoons so clearly that it is almost like playing a videotape in my head. I used to do that and then make the sound effects along with the story in my head. Other kids heard me making those noises and thought I was nuts. But I didn't know they thought that. I didn't know other kids were able to think about me because I couldn't think about them.

The thing I hated most in junior high was being teased. That was even worse than the homework. Mean kids used to try to upset me by imitating me or trying to get me in trouble. They thought it was funny that I was so "weird." They wanted me to act even stranger so they could laugh at me. I knew they were being mean to me, but never could understand exactly what was happening. Sometimes I got so frustrated that I just "lost it" and threw a fit. I didn't know that was what the mean kids wanted me to do.

Sometimes nice kids would try to help me when I got confused. I could usually tell who was really trying to help me, but I'm not sure how. I almost never can remember other people's names, but I sometimes could remember the names of the nice kids. Most of the teachers in junior high tried to help me. But even some of the teachers felt uncomfortable around me because I was so different.

In both grade school and junior high my mom came to school at the beginning of each year and talked to both the students and teachers about me and autism. I think that helped everyone understand me better. I especially liked it when she talked about all the things I am good at. I noticed the teasing was less once the other kids understood autism better and its affect on me. My teachers often knew very little about autism before they met me. The additional information from my mom made the teachers more comfortable dealing with me and gave them ideas on how to help me learn.

My ability to handle my life has gotten better as I grew up. All through high school I went to regular classes by myself without an aid. I also started riding the regular school bus. I have a resource room in the high school, but I don't use it very much. I do all my own homework in my high school and college courses. (My parents haven't even been able to understand my math homework since I was in the fifth grade.)

I'm not sure how, but being autistic has made it really easy for me to learn math. I am studying areas of math now that most math teachers do not understand. (—slight pause.)

I have always had trouble understanding how other people think. Because of this, it is still almost impossible for me to lie or do magic tricks. Lying and magic involve fooling people. When you don't understand how others think, you can't fool them. Because I don't understand other people well, it is also very hard for me to make friends. I just don't know how to be friendly. For a long time, I didn't have any friends, but I do have a few close friends now. Most of them are also autistic young people. My closest friend is Chris, who plays video games with me. He often sleeps over at my house and we stay up until the middle of the night playing Nintendo 64. My friend Erin and I go to the same high school and went to Prom together last year. I think she's nice, but we don't have a lot in common. She likes dancing a lot, but it just isn't my thing. I'm not really interested in having a girlfriend and don't think I'll ever get married or have children. Right now all I really care about are computers, math, video games and hyraxes. I feel close to my mom, stepfather and sister and sometimes like to do things with them. Most of the time I prefer to be alone to pursue my interests. (—slight pause.)

I have trouble communicating, but I am very smart. My nonverbal IQ tested at 144 when I was 14. When I took a test of visual/spatial skills when I was in junior high, I scored higher than the top of the high school scale.

I was on the math team at Monona High School. As part of the team, in 1995 I took the American High School Mathematics Exam. I got the the highest score in the state of Wisconsin on this exam. As a result, I was invited to be on the Wisconsin All-State Mathematics team in 1996, 97, and 98. This math team goes to the University of Iowa each June to participate in the American Regions Mathematics League National Math Contest. In this math competition, I got no special help. Sometimes I had trouble on team questions because of my autism, but I was still able to help the team.

It's a little easier for me to communicate with others about math because I understand it so well and like it so much. The other "math nerds" on the team seemed to accept my odd parts better than most people. I don't look so different in a group of teenagers where everyone has a pocket protector and a giant calculator in their back pocket.

I work very hard in school. My favorite subjects are math and science. All through junior and senior high I have gotten mostly A's and B's on my report cards. I have a 3.23 overall grade point average for high school. I scored high enough on the advanced placement test for math that I could have skipped the first two semesters of college calculus. Instead, I only skipped the first semester and enrolled in a second semester honors calculus course at the UW. I earned an A/B in third semester calculus and am taking linear algebra this semester.

Even though I have trouble communicating, I enjoyed the two years of Spanish I took in high school. I was fascinated by the conjugation of Spanish verbs and wore out my first copy of a Spanish dictionary.

Sometimes people ask how I get along with my sister, Liz. I'm glad I have Liz for a sister, but she's ten years younger than I am. Mom says it's like she has two "only" children. Besides the age gap, our interests are very different. She loves Beanie Babies; I think Beanie Babies are useless. We don't fight much, mostly because we don't spend much time together. Sometimes I get bothered when Liz hangs out in the same room where I'm doing my homework. It makes her mad when I tell her to go away. Liz thinks I worry about too many things. Sometimes we fight about what to watch on TV, but more often Liz and I team up to get our parents to turn on Nickelodeon. Liz and I also work together to get Mom and Dad to take us to McDonald's. (—slight pause.)

I have lots of interests and hobbies. My first major interest when I was three years old was stairways and escalators. I especially liked curved stairways and would look for them and climb them wherever I went. Since then, I have intensely studied many other things. I consider myself an expert in gear assemblies, Lego construction toys, spirograph drawing equipment and several Nintendo games.

I taught myself origami when I was nine. With the help of various origami books, I graduated from cranes to other figures. I can now make many kinds of animals and the most complex geometric models. I like the geometric models best because they have more math and are more interesting to look at. I have some of my origami work here to show you.

My current major interests are fractals, Nintendo video games and hyraxes. Fractals involve the computerized generation of fractal graphics pictures, based on mathematical chaos theory. I have software on my computer that is designed to solve mathematical equations and then translate the results into computer graphics. These graphics are "chaotic" in the mathematical sense in both form and color. I have some fractal pictures with me to show you. I enjoy making up complex equations and plugging the results into the software. I have two computers. One is a portable that I take with me. I like to show people my fractal images and talk about them.

Hyraxes are small mammals from Southern Africa. I am trying to learn everything I can about them. I have also made up stories about my imaginary world where people and hyraxes live together. I have a report here about hyraxes as a handout to show you.

Besides the things listed above, I have also been fascinated by pterodactyls, ferrets, elevators, Disney cartoons, interstate highways, *Mad Magazine*, Bart Simpson, Garfield, Calvin and Hobbes, Charlie Chaplin, the Three Stooges, the Marx Brothers, Pink Panther movies, race car crashes, South Park cartoons and hairless dogs. I have a Chinese Crested (hairless) dog named Beijing. Having a dog has made me more aware of things outside myself. (—slight pause.)

Like most autistic people, I am constantly struggling to communicate. The frustrations of this struggle often make me feel tense and nervous. My language is quite good, but talking is stressful because it takes a lot of effort for me. My voice often sounds "funny." I have very few friends because of my communication problems. There are little things about the way I move and the tone of my voice that signal to you NT's (Neural Typical People) that I am "different."

It is easier for me to talk when I can read the words. That's why I am able to give these speeches. One of the good things about being autistic is I'm never embarrassed to speak in front of large crowds. In 1996, I addressed the Legislative Joint Finance Committee in Madison. I've also spoken at conferences, other training sessions and to university classes about autism. The last thing my mom expected was to see me on the "speaker's circuit," but here I am.

It is also painful for me to look at other people's faces. Other people's mouths and eyes are especially hard for me to look at. My lack of "eye contact" sometimes makes people (especially teachers) think I am not paying attention to them. I have been working with my mom and my teachers to come up with ways to manage this eye contact problem. This includes letting people know about this problem if they will be working with me a lot. I have also been practicing looking near people's faces rather than right at them or looking at them for a second or two and then looking away when I start to feel uncomfortable.

I do hear and usually understand when people are talking to me even if I don't look at them. However, it takes longer than average for me to process and understand things I hear. It also takes longer for me to figure out what to reply and then to say it. When people talk to me, it helps a lot if they speak slowly and give me time to respond without pressuring me.

A few people have really "gotten in my face" and yelled at me in an attempt to get me to respond to them. This only makes things worse. This type of pressure causes my thought processes to "crash" like an overworked computer disk. It's like all my thoughts are trying to get out of my head at once and I can't deal with it.

I have developed various strategies to deal with stress. Some of these things upset other people (especially my teachers) because they didn't understand why I did them. And I couldn't communicate well enough to explain things, even to myself. For example, my parents said I banged my head a lot when I got frustrated when I was young. But I usually banged it on soft things so it didn't hurt much. Sometimes when I am mad now, I still swing my head through the air. But I don't hit anything with my head. Head banging motions help me deal with nervousness.

I also usually have some books, pictures and some type of electronic equipment like a computer, calculator, or Gameboy with me wherever I go. These things remind me of home, which is a safe place for me. When I'm home, I usually can do whatever I want. Except when I have to clean my room or unload the dishwasher. Having my special things with me makes me feel calmer and helps me deal with stress.

I also take three medications to help me cope. I have been taking Ritalin since I was seven. I now take it five times a day and it helps me be more in control. I have also taken Zoloft, a relative of Prozac, for the past four years. The Zoloft seems to help calm me and helps me stop worrying about little things. I also started taking Propranolol this year to help calm me, because the Zoloft seems less effective than it used to be. Many older autistic people take drugs like Zoloft or Prozac because they are effective against the obsessive/compulsive tendencies which often occur with autism. (—slight pause.)

Like most autistic people I have problems with my senses. Sudden, loud noises are very stressful for me. Especially things like gunshots, loud motors and chain saws. My mom took me through a drive-in car wash once when I was in grade school, and I was terrified. The brushes sounded to me like the sound of machine gun fire. Just looking at the whirling motion of the brushes frightened me, but I couldn't communicate well enough then to explain why I got so upset.

Over the years, I managed to train myself to tolerate some problem noises. But the possibility of unexpected loud noises is a constant source of low-level anxiety for me. However, my auditory sensitivity has gotten a lot better since I had auditory integration training when I was 14 and again when I was 17. Auditory training has helped me a lot. I think parents of autistic children should give it a try, especially if the child is sensitive to noise.

But not all autistic people have the same problems. When I was a baby, I wouldn't eat anything with lumps in it because I hated texture. Some autistic people won't wear some types of clothing because of the way it feels. Temple Grandin, a famous autistic person I know, has a severe touch sensitivity. She has to wash new shirts about five times before she can stand to wear them. She described the sensation of new clothing as being like "using toilet paper made out of sandpaper." Her only way of letting her parents know how painful new dresses were before she could talk, was to scream hysterically when she was being dressed for church. It is common for me and other autistic people to be unable to say the words to describe what is bothering us. It's also hard for us to figure out that other people don't experience the world the same way we do.

I don't think I have a lot of unusual problems with my sight, taste, touch or balance. However, I hate the feeling of "static electricity" and seem especially sensitive to its presence. I also like my special glasses that my parents got for me as an experiment. They have Irlen lenses which are designed to help filter out disturbing light patterns. (—slight pause.)

I enjoy my part-time job shelving books at the UW Memorial Library. I worked there 20 hours a week this past summer. Before that, I did similar work at the Monona Public Library for three years. The best things about my job is that it is quiet there, and I don't have to talk with people very often. I memorize things like library filing systems very quickly so the job is quite easy for me. I also helped out in the early childhood classroom in my high school. I like talking to little kids and helping them with things like zipping their coats.

Last year I learned to ride the city buses. I have a very good memory for things like bus routes, so I can get around the whole city by myself now. I ride the city bus from Monona High to my UW class and back by myself every day.

I got my temporary driver's license last year. My parents never thought I'd learn to drive because of my autism. Some of the professionals in the autism community convinced my mom to give me a chance to try driving. It helped when I found out I could handle a go-cart real well. Besides that, I'm a wizard at driving video games. I need a lot more practice, but I'm hoping to get my license some day. When I first started practicing driving it was pretty scary. Now only my parents are scared. (—slight pause.)

In the summer of 1997 I took a study skills class called College Success at MATC in Madison. It was a regular three-credit class collapsed into five weeks. I had an aid in class with me the first week.

The teacher teamed me with another student to keep me on track for the rest of the class. The class was well organized and the materials were good. The bad news is that it was not a college success for me. I got a "D" in that class. The first "D" I ever got on a report card. I had a lot of trouble with the fast pace of the class. I never had a class before where I had a whole chapter of homework on the first day. Also, the class focused on things like relationships and future planning. These have always been things that I have a hard time understanding and thinking about.

I think I could do a lot better if I took that class again with more time to study. The class was still a valuable learning experience. It also shows how someone with a disability like autism can have trouble learning even though they're smart, have lots of support and are trying hard.

I would like to get a math degree from the University of Wisconsin. Although I have more than enough credits to graduate from high school, I am still in high school because I need help with transition and community skills. (—slight pause. —look up.)

As teachers, remember that not all autistic people are the same. Lots of autistic people can carry on conversations easier than I can and not all autistic people are good at math. Most autistic people certainly never give speeches like I do. Watch carefully for possible sensory issues with your students. Sensory problems can cause behavior problems, but are often overlooked. I didn't even tell my teachers about my sensory problems because I didn't know my senses were different. I just thought everyone else had figured out how to cope better. All people with special needs are people first, and deserve to be respected as individuals.

Being autistic is part of who I am. Sometimes I have problems but I am satisfied with my life. I enjoy my hobbies and am proud of my accomplishments. I know there's a place for my special talents if I can just find it. Being able to read speeches like this makes me feel like I finally have a voice of my own. Thank you for listening to me.

My mom is here with me today as my facilitator/interpreter and to give you additional information about autism and me. After my mom's comments, I would welcome the opportunity to answer any questions you have. It is good verbal practice for me. Please give me at least ten seconds to reply. If I am having trouble understanding your question, I may ask my mom for assistance.

[Note: Matthew Ward is available for speaking engagements. For contact information, see Appendix, page 150.]

Quotable Quotes

To truly know another human being and their experience of the world is one of the greatest gifts we can receive. Because we want to help you understand what it is like to live with autism, that experience is clearly best communicated by those who actually live it themselves. We gain one of our clearest glimpses from this first-hand account of autism by J. R. Bemporad (1979): "Nothing seemed constant. Everything appeared to be always changing."

From those two short sentences we are given a quick and powerful look into what it is like when you have autism. Since Bemporad's early writings, more and more individuals with autism have shared their perceptions of the world with us. One of the best known of these individuals is Temple Grandin. Temple has written books, presented papers and prepared speeches that have been shared worldwide, helping all of us gain a clearer perspective of what it is like to live with the challenges of autism spectrum disorders.

Below we have gathered a variety of quotations from such individuals. Sharing these quotes can serve as a springboard for as brief or as detailed a discussion as you might want to have about what it is like to have autism and the difficulties associated with it. Sometimes we have shared them as a handout, and sometimes we have posted them on large posterboards around the room to help all of us wanting to support such individuals keep their experiences and perspectives ever present in our minds.

An especially effective use of the quotations is to have members of a class/audience read them aloud to one another. Speaking and hearing first-person insights can bring the experience of autism more fully to life, and can be an important first step in our journey of learning to walk awhile in their autism. We are grateful to all of those who have been open in sharing who they are and their unique perceptions:

"My hearing is like having a sound amplifier set on maximum loudness. My ears are like a microphone that picks up and amplifies sound. I have two choices: 1) turn my ears on and get deluged with sound or 2) shut my ears off."
(Temple Grandin)

"When my mom moved the furniture in the house I got very, very upset. I hated the change. I felt like I was not at home any more."
(Paul McDonnell)

"I loved repetition. Every time I turned on a light I knew what would happen. When I flipped the switch, the light went on. It gave me a wonderful feeling of security because it was exactly the same each time."
(Sean Barron)

"I felt secure in 'my world' and hated anything that tried to call me out of there ... People, no matter how good, had no chance to compete."
(Donna Williams)

"I learned to talk at 4. I didn't learn to communicate until 11 or 12."
(Bill Donovan)

"I simply didn't know ... what talking was for ... Speech therapy was just a lot of meaningless drills in repeating meaningless sounds for incomprehensible reasons. I had no idea that this could be a way to exchange meaning with other minds."
(Jim Sinclair)

"I remember my mother telling me not to do things I loved. My parents were always interrupting me and interfering with me."
(Sean Barron)

"I was rarely able to hear sentences because my hearing distorted them. I was sometimes able to hear a word or two at the start and understand it and then the next lot of words sort of merged into one another and I could not make head or tail of it."
(Darren White)

"I have just come from another classroom where I had been tortured by sharp white fluorescent light, which made reflections bounce off everything. It made the room race busily in a constant state of change. Light and shadow dancing on people's faces as they spoke turned the scene into an animated cartoon."
(Donna Williams)

"I just CAN'T understand human emotions, no matter how hard I try."
(Paul McDonnell)

"In the past I used to ask the same question over and over and I used to drive my parents crazy by doing that! I wanted to hear the same answer over and over because I was never sure of anything ... I wanted an exact answer to everything; uncertainty used to drive me crazy."
(Paul McDonnell)

"I wanted to understand emotions. I had dictionary definitions for most of them and cartoon caricatures of others ... I also had trouble reading what other people felt."
(Donna Williams)

"I would often talk on and on about something that interested me ... I really was not interested in discussing anything; nor did I expect answers or opinions from the other person, and I would often ignore them or talk over them if they interrupted."
(Donna Williams)

"I am like Data, the android man, on 'Star Trek, the Next Generation.' As he accumulates more information, he has a greater

understanding of social relationships. I am a scientist who has to learn the strange ways of an alien culture."
(Temple Grandin)

"When I encounter a new social situation, I have to scan my memory and look for previous experiences that were similar. As I accumulate more memories, I become more and more skilled at predicting how other people will act in a particular situation."
(Temple Grandin)

"After reading Temple Grandin's autobiography ... someone asked me if I thought a cattle chute would have helped me. I said I didn't need a cattle chute, I needed an orientation manual for extraterrestrials. Being autistic does not mean being inhuman. But it does mean being alien."
(Jim Sinclair)

"I was never quite sure how to handle certain situations. It is very difficult ... to know exactly when to say something, when to ask for help, or when to remain quiet ... Life is a game in which the rules are constantly changing without rhyme or reason."
(Anne Carpenter)

"It's not so much about winning or losing, but the process, and being able to participate."
(Jerry Newport)

"I felt like the world was an ocean and I never knew which wave was going to knock me over next."
(Jerry Newport)

"Whatever the reasons, I, as an autistic person, reacted in a fixated behavior pattern in order to reduce arousal to my overstimulated nervous system."
(Temple Grandin)

A Final Note

It can be important and powerful to include individuals with autism in teaching others about their experience of the world. It is also important to honor their perspective if they DON'T want others to know about their disability. Some people with autism may prefer not to be identified. In fact, it is the legal right of all students with disabilities to have their confidentiality protected. (See page 33 for specific confidentiality information.) In those cases, it may be helpful to do activities which focus on the overall acceptance of differences, without calling attention to the individual with autism specifically. Sometimes, the parent of a person with autism is willing to come in and talk to the class. Again, the guideline needs to be: What does this person want others to know about him/her? And, how can that information be shared respectfully to the people for whom it will be useful? A balance needs to be found by providing information that can lead to deepened understanding without overdoing it.

Consider this scenario: A student with autism was going to be entering a middle school for the first time. With permission from the parents of the student with autism, the administration—with all good intentions—pulled together the entire middle school student body and staff and shared information regarding this student. That resulted in a situation of too much information to too many people too soon. It set the student apart in a manner that wasn't helpful. Personal information about the student's behavioral and communication challenges was shared such that the peers were looking for the differences instead of getting to know him as an individual. Additionally, many students and staff whose relationship with him was limited to only occasionally passing him in the hallway had specific, personal information about him. This led to the student feeling embarrassed and self-conscious throughout the entire building. While the administrative intent was positive, the outcome was a bit disastrous.

The critical aspect when doing any kind of sensitivity training is to make certain that the manner in which the information is shared will promote relationship and understanding; not set the student apart in an unusual and/or uncomfortable fashion.

2. SENSITIZING PEERS

Because we want students with autism to be able to function without the direct support of an adult whenever possible, it is sometimes necessary for us to facilitate, at least initially, their relationships with peers. As we have noted, one important aspect of "relationship" is the knowledge of how another person experiences the world.

The following activities have been developed with the idea that the more a peer understands about the perceptions and experiences of a classmate with autism, the more sensitive that peer is likely to become. These activities can help to create a compassionate and safe learning environment in which relationships can develop. To assist peers to "walk awhile in autism," the activities are designed to be as experiential as possible.

Student Survey

Prior to conducting an experiential sensitivity activity, it can be useful to obtain a sense of what the classmates' questions and perceptions are regarding the student in their class who has autism. Following are some questions developed by a teacher, Gail Stark, that could be used as a student survey to assist practitioners in planning and determining which activities to employ with a specific group of classmates. (See page 149 in the Appendix for a blank survey form which can be reproduced.)

1. You have had the opportunity to be with (student's name) for about (amount of time). What questions do you have about him and/or his abilities? What are you curious about? What would you like to know about (student's name) and/or autism?

2. How do other kids treat (student's name) in the cafeteria, hallway, classroom, bus, etc.? Are they helpful, nice, kind, mean? Do some people just ignore him? Do people seem afraid of him?

3. What do you think YOU can do to help (student's name) feel more comfortable and fit in more for the amount of time he is in your class? (Examples: greet him daily, invite him to join your group, invite him to try to remain with the activity, offer to photocopy your notes for him to study from, etc.)

While some practitioners have found such a survey helpful, others have simply asked the group with whom they are working to write out or ask aloud the questions they may have about an individual and their autism. Even preschoolers and kindergartners have questions that can be helpful in guiding sensitivity presentations. Here are some examples:

• How does he handle his problem in life?

• Is autism a disease?

• Will he be able to ride a bike?

• What do I do when he spits on me?

• How does John think?

• Why does he only have one friend?

• Why does he get nervous when things change?

A Note About Confidentiality

Students with an identified exceptional educational need (EEN) have their confidentiality protected by federal and state law. In the state of Wisconsin, the Department of Public Instruction provides the following interpretation of the confidentiality laws (Pawlisch 1998, 3):

> In general, a school district may disclose personally identifiable information from pupil records only after obtaining a signed and dated written consent from a parent. The consent must specify the records that may be disclosed; state the purpose of the disclosure; and identify the party to whom the disclosure will be made. The department recommends that the consent state the time period during which disclosure will be permitted.

Interpretations may vary from state to state. Be sure to consult your local education agency. When conducting student surveys and subsequent sensitivity trainings, it is wise to obtain written consent from the parents/guardians of the child with autism. This practice promotes good communication between school and home and also helps to avoid any unfortunate misunderstandings about what and how specific information about a student will be shared with peers and staff.

At the conclusion of a presentation to a group, or some time after, it can also be helpful to conduct a follow-up survey. This survey might ask students/classmates to complete a scale which can measure their perceptions and how they may have changed as a result of the sensitivity experiential activity. Students might be asked what additional information they may need or want. This information can guide future planning and activities for the group of classmates.

Experiential Activities

Activity #1: Visualization

"I always loved the saying, 'Stop the world, I want to get off.' Perhaps I'd been caught up in the spots and the stars at a time when other children kept developing, and so I had been left behind. The stress of trying to catch up and keep up often became too much, and I found myself trying to slow everything down and take some time out. Something would always call me back."
(Williams 1992, 45)

"I became aware that people used language to communicate with one another, but I didn't know how this was done ... I felt like an alien from outer space—I had no more idea how to communicate with people than a creature from another planet."
(Barron & Barron 1992, 197-198)

Description:

Guided visualizations can be a powerful way to help some individuals begin to create an experience for themselves without actually having the experience itself (Groden et al. 1989). There is nothing we can do to truly create the experience of autism for someone who doesn't have autism. However, in this activity the teacher/facilitator reads or speaks a visualization that takes the participants on a trip through their imagination that is designed to bring them closer to our understanding of autism.

The teacher/facilitator begins by asking the participants to get into a position that is comfortable for them. This may be sitting in chairs for some, on the floor for others. Tell them that you will be lowering the lights, then asking them to engage their imagination to join you on a special kind of trip. Let them know that some people find that closing their eyes makes the experience seem even more real, and invite them to do that if they feel comfortable. Instruct them to take a couple of deep cleansing breaths to prepare for the trip, then pause for 15-30 seconds of silence. Begin reading or speaking in an even and calm tone, taking the participants through the visualization.

After slowly and gently bringing them back to the present moment and present space, facilitate a discussion beginning with what their direct experience of the "trip" was like. Have several people share. Relate their visualization experience to the characteristics seen in people with autism. Reference their classmate with autism or reports by other individuals with autism.

Setting it up:

Explain to the participants that we all have different ways in which we experience the world, and that we are going to help them use their imagination to take a trip to a place where their experiences of the world are different than the ones they have here on Planet Earth.

You will need:

Room enough for people to be comfortable and relaxed.

One of the following visualization scripts:

Planet Autism

I'm going to take you on an intergalactic trip, if you are willing. No spaceship is required because we will be using the magnificent energy of our minds to transport us instantaneously to our destination. It is only necessary to close your eyes, find a comfortable collection of quiet thoughts, and open your thinking to the strange new world that is appearing at the center of your consciousness.

We have just landed on an uncharted planet where your assignment is to "fit in." Your initial perceptions are of unfocused noise and movement, but you sense a familiarity to the lifeforms taking shape before your eyes. These aliens appear very similar to you. For a moment you study them closely, you watch the way they move, the way they stand, the way they sit. And then you study your own physical form in order to make some comparison. You watch how your body moves. Your hands dance in front of your face and shimmer like the wings of birds. You have a vision of your body flying gracefully through the air.

You close your eyes for a moment and you feel your body floating and floating. When you reopen your eyes you see a collection of inanimate objects, shapes, and forms that lie quietly at your feet, and they bring you comfort because their stillness is easy to comprehend. You begin to interact with these objects, some of which are round, some of which are square, and you find serenity in your ability to pick them up, to move and rearrange them.

But now the aliens have reappeared, and they capture your focus once again.

They seem to be asking something. Their voices make you anxious because the words are confusing. These individuals are very persistent in their desire to interact with you, and there are occasional moments of clarity when the words make sense. However, many times the words are only noise and even though you want to be helpful, you don't know what to do. You try to focus all of your concentration on the words, but it doesn't help. In fact, sometimes it makes the confusion worse, so you look away when the aliens confront you. [Pause.]

Now you are frustrated. You want to connect with them and find a common ground of communication. It has become clear that they are identical to you in many, many ways. You want them to understand the difficulty you are experiencing in trying to please them, and in trying to make your own needs known. You want them to understand that you speak a very similar language, but you are visiting a strange planet with a different atmosphere and your body is not working the way you want it to. Most of all, you want them to understand that you're not stupid or slow; in fact, you are expending tremendous amounts of energy trying to break through the wall of noise and chaos that seems to fill the very air that you are breathing.

Out of desperation, you begin to mimic their gestures, and they seem pleased with your effort. But after a while they grow tired of your mimicry and they respond with hostility and anger. You try again and again to use words and gestures to speak their language, but the frustration now is growing among all of you, and you realize that you have yourself become a part of the noise and the chaos.

You just want to find a space in which to be alone. You seek the comfort of your own arms moving before your eyes and you find solace in arranging the objects at your side. Sometimes you experiment with spinning yourself around. You extend the spinning to the objects in your reach. You line them up, spin them around, or allow them to be still. You discover immense satisfaction in having control over your environment. You repeat the movements and gestures and patterns that feel the most pleasing to your body and mind.

After a time, some of the words and behaviors that had met with approval from the aliens come back to you and you repeat them to yourself. You find yourself missing the company of these individuals who are so much like you, so you return your attention to them and you try once again to connect and to fit in.

They like that. Their anger having dissolved, they try to help.

They try to help by touching you. But the touch does not always feel helpful; in fact, sometimes it feels like an electric shock surging through your entire body. You realize now that your senses work very differently on this planet. Some of the time you don't seem to be able to feel, hear, or smell much at all, and at other times these same sounds, feelings and smells are distracting or even painful. But despite this, you keep trying to connect for the simple reason that your mind is filled with observations you are desperate to share: love and hate, frustration and joy.

For younger audiences (i.e., 5-12 years), you may want to use the following version:

Planet Autism

Okay, get ready, because if you're willing, I'm going to take you on a very interesting trip. I'm going to take you to another planet, but you don't need a spaceship. You're going to be traveling using the magnificent energy of your mind and your imagination. I don't know exactly when we will be leaving yet, so settle in for a bit with some comfortable thoughts, and I'll let you know as soon as I receive the go ahead from the captain.
[Pause here for 15-30 seconds.]
That's it! I've received the go-ahead. I am transporting you immediately to a new planet we have just discovered. You will be here for ... oh, I don't know how long. Until the captain says to bring you back. While you are here, your main assignment is to try to connect with the beings that live here and to "fit in" as best you can.
At first you have a hard time figuring out what it is you are hearing and what it is you are seeing. Things are clear for a bit, then they suddenly get fuzzy. Then, without any warning, they are clear again. Yet from the beginning, you sense something familiar about the life-forms taking shape before your eyes. These aliens appear very similar to you.
For a moment you study them closely, you watch the way they move, the way they stand, the way they sit. You try to understand the sounds that are coming from ... are those ... their faces? And then

you study your own body to see how hard or easy it's going to be to connect with them and to "fit in." You watch how your body moves. Your hands dance in front of your face and shimmer like the wings of birds, splitting the light into shooting and swirling designs. You move about with total freedom, sometimes smoothly, and sometimes crashing into the things around you.

You look around more closely for a moment, at all the things surrounding you. In addition to the aliens, you notice lots and lots of things that don't move around so much. Some of the things are round, some have corners, some are flat, some are soft, and some are hard. What are all these things? You line them all up in a row. There. These things are easier to deal with than the aliens. They only move when you want them to, and you can control how they move. Oh, look at how you can make them all spin!

But now the aliens have come back, and you remember ... you're supposed to try to connect and "fit in." They come close to you. You hear those noises they make again. They seem to be asking you something. You try to make sense of the noises, but it's really hard. But they keep making them, and after a while, you start to understand what some of the noises mean. You get it. They want you to do things like them. They want you to make the same kinds of noises. You try. You try really hard, and sometimes you get it right. Oh, they get so excited when that happens. But sometimes you try just as hard and you just can't get your body to work the way you want. They are not so happy then. Sometimes the only way to get a break is to look away from them. [Pause.]

They keep trying and you keep trying to connect. You see that you are so much like each other in so many ways. And you want them to understand that you want to do what they ask, that you want to be able to talk with them. You just can't always make your body do what you want or find the words you want to speak. You really want them to understand that you're not stupid or slow; in fact, you are expending tremendous amounts of energy trying to break through the wall of noise and chaos that seems to fill the very air that you are breathing on this planet you are visiting.

To fulfill your mission of "fitting in," you keep doing what they are doing and saying what they are saying. But they don't seem as happy with you for doing that as they did before. After a while they grow tired of you doing what they do, and they even get angry.

When this happens, you just want to find a space in which to be alone. You start moving your hands before your eyes again, then you start lining up all the objects at your side. Sometimes you do the spinning thing again, too. And this time, you start spinning your body as well. You do all of these things over, and over, and over for a while.

Then you remember ... fit in. And besides, you kind of miss the aliens when they are not around. So you seek them out and try again. They like that, and they try to help. They try to help by touching you. But the touch does not always feel helpful; in fact, sometimes it feels like an electric shock surging through your entire body. Then an interesting thing happens. They learn to touch you differently. There ... that's better. They slow down. There ... that's easier. They're working hard to be with you ... that feels better. You start to find each other's rhythm. You shift, they shift. It's starting to work. Sometimes you manage to "fit in" a bit better, and when you don't ... you know they still like you anyway ... and they won't leave you alone.

This is what I have come to call my filter of autism. Bring it back with you now as you return to this room. Keep it handy as we begin to talk about how we can help people with autism feel more at home.

As Christian Morgenstern wrote: "Home is not where you live, but where they understand you."

Major points to make:

√ Feelings of disorientation can be common for some people with autism.

√ Being able to "connect" and "fit in" can be challenging for many people with autism.

√ A sensory system which functions differently can make the world a very unpredictable, anxiety-producing, frustrating place in which to exist.

√ A sensory system which functions differently can make communication difficult.

√ Not being able to communicate as easily or in the same way as you or I is not the same as not wanting to communicate.

√ Challenging behavior, or behavior that is different from how we behave is usually happening for a reason, and often it is because things are scary or confusing.

√ Connecting with one another, feeling accepted and knowing there are others to support you when you need it is important for everyone.

Activity #2: The Gift Box

"Dissertation participant Jean Paul (interview) identifies with this. He says, 'I don't need to be cured. I am pretty happy with what I deal with even its, yeah, maybe it brought me challenges in my life but they are my challenges that I've dealt with and I'm pretty proud of it ... I've heard we're going to try and make a normal child out of you. There's something wrong with you, we must fix it. I don't think I need to be fixed. I don't think that it's necessarily my problem. The problem lies with the society that's intolerant of differences, like ours is ... *No one has all the insights on autism, not even those of us who experience it every day.*'"
(Emphasis added; Strandt-Conroy 1999, 136-137)

Description:

Given the many challenges experienced by individuals with autism, it can be difficult for some people to see the gifts they have to offer. In this activity, the teacher enters the classroom with a big gift box that is all wrapped up, and uses it to launch an introduction about the gifts each student in the class possesses and contributes.

Option One: The students then write/draw the gifts his/her classmates possess. The children are asked to share first what other classmates bring and offer to the class as a whole. Next, they are asked to identify the gifts they offer. The gift box stays in the class and the teacher periodically pulls a slip of paper out of the box and reads it. This is done for the purpose of reminding students about the gifts each possesses.

Option Two: The teacher's gift box is already filled with the gifts s/he perceives that each of the students possess. Then, the students as a whole are asked to start a "gift notebook" in which they write/draw the gifts they or other classmates possess throughout the year. The notebooks can be shared at intervals, in small groups or to the group at large.

Setting it up:

The teacher introduces the idea of the gift box, describing and giving examples (especially for younger students) of what is meant when we say someone has a gift (i.e., talent, something one is good at, something we like about a person, something a person contributes or adds to the class).

You will need:

A big giftwrapped box, with a removable lid or a set of notebooks that are or can be decorated to look like a "gift."

Small slips of paper and writing utensils (the pieces of paper may be cut in the shape of a bow, a small package, etc.).

Major points to make:

√ All classmates (including individuals with autism) have gifts, talents, special attributes to share. Part of working together in a community of any sort (such as a classroom) is to recognize, honor and celebrate what each person can bring to the group.

√ The gifts and talents we each bring are sometimes different from each other. That diversity is what makes us whole and what makes life exciting and fun.

√ Sometimes, with some people, we have to look harder for their gifts; however, they are there. Gifts might be as simple as how sweetly someone smiles when they get to talk about their favorite topic.

√ Sometimes, someone's gift can be what they help us learn about ourselves. For example, how good it feels when someone helps us learn to be patient.

√ Noticing and sharing our own gifts and the gifts of others makes for a more cohesive and joyful community experience for all.

Activity #3: Snack Mix

"Autism is something I cannot see. It stops me from finding and using my own words when I want to. Or makes me use all the words and silly things I do not want to say ... Autism cuts me off from my own body, and so I feel nothing."
(Williams 1994, 237)

"I was sure that I had feelings, but they did not seem to make the jump in my communication with others. I began to become increasingly frustrated, violent, and self-destructive."
(Williams 1992, 46)

Description:

This activity is an avenue to assist students in learning to recognize and celebrate diversity in general and the different preferences and choices in each other specifically.

Part One: The teacher/facilitator brings into the classroom the separated ingredients to make a snack mix. Each student has a chance to choose the particular mix of ingredients that they want in their individual cup, and to make their mix. Before the children can eat their snacks, they are asked to share what they have chosen. The teacher uses this as an opportunity to point out that while most people choose differently from each other, they've still all ended up with a snack mix in their individual cups. Teachers/facilitators can graph the results on the board or in some other way help the students to see all the different preferences they have and combinations they have made. Younger children might be given pictures and helped to make individual charts to use later in the discussion.

Part Two: The teacher/facilitator encourages each student to attempt to add one ingredient to their mix that they are unfamiliar with or haven't tried in the past.

Setting it up:

The students are told that they are going to participate in an activity about choices and people having different preferences. They are told to watch how even when each of us makes different choices, we can still all end up in a similar place.

You will need:

Makings for snack mix (e.g., pretzels, cereal, raisins, small candies, marshmallows, peanuts). Note: Make certain that the dietary needs and preferences (e.g., casein- and gluten-free diets) of all students are taken into account and that at least three items of choice are available to most students (again, particularly the student with autism).

Small cups.

Bowls/containers for each ingredient, with one scoop per ingredient.

Major points to make:

√ We all make different choices; just as we all chose different ingredients for our snack, we all choose different friends, different colors for our drawings, different things to do with our free time, etc. Encourage students to generate other categories of choice that result in them doing things differently from at least some others.

√ Use the above discussion as a springboard to point out the fact that we are cumulatively a metaphor for the snack mix. We represent a diverse mix of who we are, what we look like, what we're good at doing and prefer to do.

√ Everyone's mix tastes different, each individual mix tastes good to someone ... So, as in any group, everyone isn't going to like everyone, but someone is going to like each of us.

√ Each item has "value" to some of the people in the group, as each of us have traits that are valuable to the group. Therefore, as group members, we need to treat each "ingredient" in our "mix" in a respectful way. (Note: For younger children it may be helpful to make signs to hang around their necks with pictures/words of each ingredient to assist them in understanding the symbolic referent.)

√ Regarding the second part of the activity (trying a new ingredient): facilitate a discussion around the metaphor of trying new friends, recognizing new traits you may find valuable in current friendships; and recognizing that sometimes, when you're brave enough to try something new, you may discover your tastes have expanded, and you end up with a great new experience or friend.

Activity #4: Cognitive Style

"I think in pictures. Words are like a second language to me. I translate both spoken and written words into full-color movies, complete with sounds, which run like a VCR tape in my head. When somebody speaks to me, his words are instantly translated into pictures."

(Temple Grandin)

Description:

Have you ever had the experience of knowing that you should know something, but you either can't figure it out or don't remember it? Have you ever had the feeling that you should be able to figure out a problem, but that for some reason you just can't find the solution? You know it exists, but it lies out there, just beyond your reach. That is often the experience of autism, and that is the experience for many in this activity. Begin by having people look at the letters below (we usually write them on an overhead or on the chalkboard):

O T T F F S S

Next, ask what letter should come next? And why?

When we have done this with groups, often the first letter people guess is "O," with the rationale that the sequence is starting over. They hypothesize that the pattern is OOTTFFSSOOTTFFSS, etc. However, that is incorrect. After telling them they are incorrect, it is useful to also have them notice the feeling they have of being wrong and being unable to "get it." Sometimes people suggest a letter they think follows a pattern of number of angles or lines (U, I, etc.). The next letter is in fact E, followed by N, followed by T. Once people are provided with that information, some in the group begin to figure out the pattern. So, again, it is helpful to have those who haven't figured it out notice the feeling that this activity is designed to elicit.

Have you deciphered the pattern yet? If so, good for you! If not, try rote counting aloud. Now do you see it? Many people in the group are helped by this prompt. There are often still some that are not. Try touching each of the letters in the sequence as you count. (Each letter is the first letter of the number-word: **O**ne, **T**wo, **T**hree, **F**our, **F**ive, **S**ix, **S**even ...) Have the students notice again now how they are feeling and how their feelings have shifted.

Setting it up:

Begin this activity by letting people know that you are going to show them a series of letters, and that their job is to determine which letters come next. Ask them not to blurt out their answers, but to remain quiet until they are called upon to share. It is also helpful to ask those who have already seen this sequence and know the answer to please pass so that others may benefit from the learning.

You will need:

A blackboard, an overhead projector, or anything upon which to write so that the entire audience can see.

Major points to make:

√ This really is what it is like for many people with autism, trying to figure out any number of things they face in this world. Here, for the group, it's "What letter comes next?" In life, for the person with autism, it may be, "What activity comes next and what am I supposed to do in it?"

√ Often, when people with autism can't figure something out, they are ridiculed or punished for it (e.g., timed out for non-compliance; reprimanded). This is particularly true for individuals with high-functioning autism or Asperger's, as their language and other skills mislead others into thinking, "Well this is easy ... they SHOULD be able to figure this out."

√ Not being able to figure something out made many of the people in the audience feel a myriad of different emotions, e.g., frustrated, inferior, out of sync, not as smart, etc. These are the same feelings experienced by people with autism in similar situations.

√ Note that for all of them, when they were feeling frustrated or confused, they either knew how to seek assistance or they knew how to modulate their feelings (i.e., no one likely had an "outburst" of any kind). Asking for help and modulating how they express confusion and frustration can be very difficult for someone anywhere on the spectrum.

√ Note that for some people the prompt of just counting was enough for them to "get it." For others, it was not. The same holds true for people with autism. Some are helped by verbal cues; some are not. Some of them, as some of the audience, needed visual cues as well. Some will require direct instruction for some things.

√ Finally, note what happened and the differences in their feelings once they learned the strategy! Life becomes good and fun again.

Activity #5: Getting Stuck

"I think in some situations it's just harder for me not to have intrusive thoughts. Some autistic people, they say, block things out or they shut things down or whatever. My mind doesn't think—I'm not able to stop an intrusive thought or block something out unless it's something really, really, really mild—but if it's severe, it all comes in and there's no way I can stop it. I'm not able to tune out anything ... Intrusive thoughts would be nonsense syllables or something. I don't understand why this is—but if I was trying to study a foreign language or if I tried to study anything with odd-sounding words, I'd get nonsense syllables and stuff would pop in my mind and anxiety. It doesn't make a bit of sense. I don't know why it happens. [...] It takes a lot of concentration and I'm not able to process that much information at one time. [...] Like if I was in the music room and I saw a musical instrument or the record player was turned off, I would have intrusive thoughts about songs in my mind. Or if I was trying to read my geography assignment, a whole bunch of nonsense syllables would pop into my mind and would be triggered by funny-sounding names. Just stupid things like that—that wouldn't amount to a hill of beans, but I would just get this terrible anxiety and boy, I would just scream."

("Barbara," quoted in Strandt-Conroy 1999, 125-126)

"If I meant to go in one direction, my body headed in the other, my head still turned sometimes in the intended direction as my body walked blind in the compelled direction, off on a track of its own. Sometimes the compulsions screamed too loud for awareness to compete. Sometimes the awareness made me want to cut my arms and legs off, pull my tongue out, and stitch my mouth up. If not for a sense of humor I might have killed my body outright in retaliation, but I couldn't do that properly and completely with intention, except as a replay of someone else. Without choice I had come to do the only real option possible. I convinced myself

that compulsions were me and life and normality and that as long
as they were roughly functional, I wouldn't fight them too much."
(Williams 1996, 89)

Description:

A hallmark characteristic of autism is "stuckness." Persons on
the spectrum get "stuck" in thoughts, in their speech, in their movements, perceptions, postures, emotions, etc. For example, some students might repeat the same word or talk about the same thing over
and over. Another may not be able to execute a movement like walking through a doorway even when there's something very motivating
on the other side of it. Individuals with autism might get stuck in an
activity, with a person, with a set of materials, and not be able to easily transition to the next person, place or thing. This next activity is
designed to give some of the children the experience of being stuck
and others the experience of observing it.

The activity begins by establishing two groups of students.
Explain to the entire group that you will all be playing a short game
of Simon Says. How well the kids can play the game (sometimes an
issue for the younger ones), is not really critical. Take one group to
the side of the room or out into the hallway. Explain to them that you
will be playing Simon Says, and that each time you ask them to
switch to a new action, you want them to keep doing the old action
10 more times before they switch. You may have to help younger
children remember to "stay stuck" the first couple of times. As
Simon, direct the kids through 3-5 activities.

After the game is over, have the children take a few deep breaths
to help them return to a state of calm and focus. Then lead a discussion around their noticings, beginning with the group who experienced being stuck. Talk to the students who were "stuck" about
whether they liked being stuck or not. Some usually do, and some
don't. Ask the children in the other group what kinds of things they
thought about their friends who were stuck. Some usually think they
looked silly, and some peers might feel sorry for them. Honor all
comments at this point, looking for how to work them into the dis-

cussion of how to be more compassionate and understanding when we see our friends with autism in a place of "stuckness."

Setting it up:

Divide students into two groups. Explain that you will all be playing a short game of Simon Says. Cue one group to "get stuck" as you are playing.

You will need:

Space enough to play Simon Says safely.

Major points to make:

√ Many of our friends on the autism spectrum experience getting stuck every day.

√ Some of our friends with autism get stuck in physical movements, just like the group playing the game and pretending to be stuck. People with autism often can't choose to become "unstuck."

√ Sometimes, friends with autism may get stuck in ways that aren't physical, like stuck in thoughts, words, postures, or emotions.

√ Sometimes, even for our friends on the spectrum, it isn't fun to be stuck.

√ Sometimes our friends with autism are laughed at for being stuck, and that probably doesn't feel good to them.

√ Sometimes it feels good to be stuck, or helps the person who is stuck to calm down if they are nervous about something.

This discussion can then be continued by teaching the students about ways to help when their friends with autism are stuck. Examples: physical touch; visual supports; relaxation; compassion.

Activity #6: The Sensory Experience of Autism

"I believe that my apraxia involves certain messages being sent to the brain and then, in turn, to different parts of my body. I cannot seem to tell my right from my left although I know my right from my left. I cannot seem to find my mouth upon command. I have trouble finding where my nose is when I am asked. I find that my breath will not come when I am asked to blow or when I am asked to take a deep breath. I am unable to draw through a straw. I have trouble sticking out my tongue. I cannot seem to spit the water out when brushing my teeth. I cannot purse my lips when I want to drink out of a bottle. I don't seem to get the message to wave or to smile when I should be responding to someone or something. My autism seems to be apparent in my random use of my hands and feet. My habit of biting is a symptom of my being nonverbal and is mostly due to frustration."

(Hale & Hale 1999, 60)

Description:

In the next set of activities we explain ways to teach others about the sensory experience of having autism. It is most helpful to begin the activities with #6, The Sensory Experience of Autism, in order to set the stage for the subsequent discussions regarding sensory processing and integration. Each of the sub-activities addresses a specific sensory experience that is common to individuals with autism (Gillingham 1995; Grandin 1986; Kranowitz 1998; Myles et al. 2000). While all of Activity #6 and the sub-activities do not need to occur during the same block of time, it is useful to do the introducing activity and then follow it up with at least some of the sub-activities. It is useful to choose sub-activities that illuminate the particular sensory characteristics that the classmate with autism experiences.

While we recognize that it is impossible to exactly simulate the range of experiences of individuals with autism spectrum disorder, we believe it is useful for students and staff alike to come as close as they can to having those experiences themselves. Having this shared perspective can increase compassion for and understanding and acceptance of individuals who live similar experiences every day of their lives. This activity provides students/staff with a number of different opportunities to "walk awhile" in autism.

Setting it Up:

Begin with a drawing of the brain on the board or on an overhead. Explain that there is an ever growing body of research that is showing us how the brains of individuals with autism spectrum disorders function uniquely. That's important, because it's how our brain functions that makes certain experiences hard or easy for us. It makes different kinds of learning harder or easier for us, and it makes how well we can help others understand what we need and want hard or easy. Ask the audience to generate different ways in which the brain gets information for learning about and experiencing the world. Again, remember ... accept any answer that is given, even if it not an answer you were wanting. Then either ask the question again, or reframe the question. For example, when doing this activity, many students often answer that one way we learn is from books. Tell them yes, that's true, we do learn from books. Then have them tell you how your brain gets the information that is in books, leading them to identifying sight as one of the ways the brain receives information.

The class/audience will usually generate the senses of sight, hearing, touch, smell, and taste. From here, talk about how messages from the world come to our brains through these senses, indicating on your drawing, a smooth message being sent. Point out that for most of us, most of the time, messages come in this smoothly. Again, using your drawing, show how messages coming in to individuals with autism are sometimes different. Sometimes they come in as if they are stronger than you and I perceive them. At other times, the messages may not come in strongly enough; they may get interrupted or distorted, or they may be totally blocked by other messages (because other messages are too strong or because the individual can process only one kind of message at a time).

Spend some time pointing out that the brain receives messages and sends messages out to the body so that we can intersect with the world and other people in it. And that just like the messages coming in, for people with autism, the messages going out to their bodies are not always smooth and consistent (Donnellan and Leary 1995). This can result in some very different experiences for all of us.

Next, let the audience choose which sense they would like to explore first, then proceed with the following corresponding experience ...

Activity #6a: Differences in Hearing

"Because other people's sound processing was alien to me, I had no idea that sound should not be like a pressure-cooker lid. I put my hands to my ears for loud sudden noises, but the continuous clamor of everyday life was only relieved by movement. Even in the classroom there was visual stimulation and noise, which combined with my own breathing and a buzzing effect that I think was my own inner ear. I rocked, swayed and scampered, even though I knew how to sit in one place and that it was expected of me. I could provide my own stimulation by running round and round the little tables."

(Blackman 1999, 51)

"Intensely preoccupied with the movement of the spinning coin or lid, I saw nothing or heard nothing. People around me were transparent. And no sound intruded on my fixation. It was as if I were deaf. Even a sudden loud noise didn't startle me from my world."

(Grandin & Scariano 1986, 18-19)

"I could only comprehend about five to ten percent of what was said to me unless I repeated the words to myself. The security of having time and space to wrestle with the relative importance or significance of spoken words was so unreachable as to not even be worth dreaming about."

(Williams 1994, 97)

"Sometimes people would have to repeat a particular sentence several times for me, as I would hear it in bits, and the way in which my mind had segmented their sentence into words left me with a strange and sometimes unintelligible message. It was a bit like when someone plays around with the volume switch on the TV.

"Similarly my response to what people said to me would often be delayed as my mind had to take time to sort out what they had

said. The more stress I was under, the worse it became."
(Williams 1992, 69)

Experience 1: Loud and disruptive sound

Setting it up:

Ask students to get out paper and something with which to write. Tell them you are going to give them a spelling test. (For kindergartners, tell them you want them to draw pictures of some items you will name.) Turn the radio on as loud as it will go, or turn the volume control back and forth so that the radio is alternating loud and soft. As you present the words to be spelled or the items to be drawn, lower the volume of your own voice. Ignore any noticings or complaints students may have. After presenting four or five items in this manner, stop. Ask students to share what that experience was like for them.

You will need:

A radio that can be turned loud enough to interfere, paper and pencils/crayons/markers for students.

Major points to make:

√ This was an example of how hearing might work for some people with autism.

√ For some people with autism, the regular noise of the classroom can be like the loud radio.

√ For some people with autism, the way they hear voices is like this experience. They can hear voices clearly and understand them some of the time, and then suddenly, without any warning, they can no longer hear or understand the words of others.

√ Help students notice that with this kind of interference, even if they knew how to spell the word or draw the picture, they probably couldn't. This happens for people with autism all the time. They know how to do something, but can't because of the interference.

√ Talk about what some people with autism might do when things are too loud for them, the way the radio was too loud here. (Some will cover their ears, some with put their fingers in their ears, some will run away, some will scream, etc.)

Experience 2: Sudden and intense sounds

Setting it up:

Have students pretend to be taking a rest (have them put their heads down on their desks and close their eyes if they are comfortable enough to do so). Dim the lights and put on some quiet music. As you are talking to the students and helping them notice how nice it feels to be calm and relaxed, have someone else from somewhere else in the room pop a balloon or sound a loud buzzer or foghorn. Pretend you didn't notice it and continue talking. Ignore their noticings. Have the sound repeated. Again, ignore the sound and their noticings. Say a few more things to try to keep them relaxed. Then share with them that you now know what they were hearing and point out its source. Have the sound made again. Then tell the person making the sound to do it only one more time, on the count of three. Count and have the sound produced again. Lead a discussion of people's reactions to this experience.

You will need:

Some quiet music and a way in which to play it. Something that will create a loud and brief sound (balloons to pop, foghorn, whistle, gong, etc.).

Major points to make:

√ For many people with autism, even the sounds of our voices can be as startling and hard to hear as the sounds you just heard.

√ For people with autism who are easily startled by sound in the way you just were, it becomes as hard for them to continue to pay attention or do an activity as it was for you to continue to relax.

√ Being startled by sound over and over can make some people with autism nervous and frightened as it did some of you.

√ Knowing where the sound is coming from, even when it's loud, can sometimes help some people.

√ Knowing when the sound is going to come can sometimes help some people.

Experience 3: Distorted sound

Setting it up:

Tell the students that you are going to play the radio and that you want them to listen very carefully. Tell them that when they hear a full sentence spoken (for kindergartners, three words in a row), you want them to raise their hand. Turn the radio on, changing the channel so frequently that it is not possible to identify a sentence (or hear three words in a row). Discuss this experience with the group.

You will need:

Radio.

Major points to make:

√ Point out that for some students with autism the sounds of other people's voices go in and out just like the radio channels were going in and out for them.

√ Help students notice the effect that this kind of hearing might have on their ability to follow directions, have a conversation, and learn when the teaching is only talking (i.e., without visual support or gesturing).

√ For some people with autism this only happens to them some of the time. So, some of the time they can hear people fine, and at other times they can't. Talk about how frustrating this can be for some of them and how some people may make the mistake of thinking that sometimes they are refusing to do things instead of not being able to understand what they are supposed to do.

Activity #6b: Losing Your Words

"At school I would walk in front of someone to get their attention and then simply begin to speak on the subject I was concerned about, usually without letting them know why I was talking about something, that would have been too direct."
(Williams 1992, 51)

"My speech really just bulges out of my mouth like a balloon, and the real thoughts in my head just keep on a direct line. The direct line and the balloon are related, but they do not correspond, and the more the balloon bulges, the less sense it makes, until it bursts, leaving nearly all my thoughts scattered, and me wild with anger and shame."
(Blackman 1999, 135)

"There are, on occasion, still times when I want to talk, but I can't. I can try and try and try, but I can't talk. There is a fear holding me back. I do not know what it is I am afraid of, I only know that it is a feeling of fear unlike any other feeling of fear I have even known. It is not that I do not want to talk, it is that I am unable to at that moment."
(McKean 1994, 39)

"Up to this time, communication had been a one-way street for me. I could understand what was being said, but I was unable to respond. Screaming and flapping my hands was my only was to communicate."
(Grandin & Scariano 1986, 17)

"Communicating with someone—anyone—continued to be a problem. I often sounded abrasive and abrupt. In my head I knew what I wanted to say but the words never matched my thoughts. I know now that not being able to follow the rhythm of another's speech was part of the problem and made me sound harsher than I intended."

(Grandin & Scariano 1986, 81)

Setting it up:

Draw a rectangle on the board or the overhead. Have the class generate a list of four words. The words do not have to be related to one another. Write the four words in the rectangle. (If you are doing this with kindergartners, draw pictures of what they say.) Next, ask for a volunteer. Tell the volunteer that you want them to pretend that they have just witnessed a very big problem that has really upset them, and they need to tell you all about it. Have them take a minute to imagine the problem, get in touch with feeling really upset, and think about what they are going to tell you. Tell them you forgot to explain that when they get upset, they have a really hard time finding their words, and that the only words they can use to tell you about the problem are the words in the rectangle. And they can't gesture with their hands.

Sometimes this restriction feels too difficult for the first volunteer. They certainly should be allowed to pass if they are uncomfortable. Pick another volunteer, then use the opportunity later to make the point that for lots of us, when things feel difficult or new, we choose not to try them. It happens for our friends on the spectrum too.

As the student tries to express the problem using only the four chosen words, do your best to try to make sense of what s/he is saying.

You will need:

A place to draw the rectangle and write the words (draw the pictures), visible to all students.

Major points to make:

√ This is what it is like for many people with autism. When they get excited or upset, it can be difficult for them to find the words they want. Sometimes they can't find any, and sometimes they can only find ones that, like the words in the rectangle, don't really help them communicate their message. Sometimes the words they can access are words that they have heard someone else say. These words may make sense or they may not. Using words they've heard before in just the same way they have heard them used is called echolalia. It can be immediate or delayed, and is usually an attempt to communicate (Prizant and Duchan 1981; Prizant 1983).

√ Often when this happens for people with autism, others who are trying to help do what happened in the example … they try to make sense out of what words the person is using. Talk about how frustrating this can be for both people involved.

√ Talk about some ways of trying to help: Staying quiet; Staying calm; Asking if you can go to where the problem is; Asking if you or the person with autism wants to try to draw what is wrong; Helping the person remember what to do to relax, which could make it easier for them to find the right words.

Activity #6c: Touch Can Feel Different

"'I'll miss you, Temple.' She walked quickly to my side and kissed my cheek. I ached to be enfolded in her arms, but how could she know? I stood rigid as a pole trapped by the approach/avoidance syndrome of autism. I drew back from her kiss, not able to endure tactile stimulation—not even loving, tactile stimulation."
(Grandin & Scariano 1986, 65)

"When I was a little older, I felt terrible walking around the house in my bare feet. It felt strange and awful to stand up and be still when I had no shoes on. My feet were extremely sensitive. So, when I had to be barefoot, I tucked my toes underneath so I could pick at the carpet with them."
(Barron & Barron 1992, 15)

"I was supersensitive to the texture of food, and I had to touch everything with my fingers to see how it felt before I could put it in my mouth."
(Barron & Barron 1992, 96)

"I felt acutely uncomfortable sitting upright in the bathtub, so I didn't enjoy taking a bath in the least. I absolutely hated the way my bottom felt against the tub, and I couldn't make myself think about something else so I wouldn't feel it. When I tried to sit normally it felt 'squishy' and I was extremely sensitive to this feeling. I couldn't shake it off. It was the same feeling I used to have when I couldn't stand to touch our rug with my bare feet. To make it more bearable, I shifted most of my weight onto one side so that only a part of me came into contact with the bathtub. When they insisted I 'sit right,' it only compounded the problem. I had no choice—I had to sit in an unnatural way, so baths were a trying experience. Also it made me feel that there was something wrong with me because I had to sit that way."
(Barron & Barron 1992, 96)

Setting it up:

Invite those who would like to participate to extend one hand and close their eyes if comfortable. Tell them you will be coming around to gently touch each one of them with the velvet glove you are wearing. Tell them you want them to notice the effect of the touch they receive, but to do their best to keep their reactions to themselves until it is time to share.

Pass through the classroom, gently touching each hand with the softness of the velvet glove. After touching all those who participated, stop and get feedback from them as to what they felt. Poll them to see how many of them liked it and how many did not. Did it make them feel calm or excited or something else?

Next, ask them to extend their hands and close their eyes again. Remind them to do their best to keep their reactions to themselves. This time, go around and touch them with the scratchy pieces of velcro that you have on the other side of the glove. After touching all those participating, ask again for their reactions, including whether they liked it, if they were surprised, etc.

You will need:

Two velvet gloves, one to be used as it is, and another to which you have attached scratchy pieces of velcro on the fingertip side of the glove.

Major points to make:

√ For some people, especially people with autism, touch that looks one way can feel very different from what you might expect (e.g., a light touch or pat might feel like a slap or a push).

√ Many people with autism have reported experiencing what we know as gentle touch as being shocking and sometimes painful. This might be why walking in busy and crowded hallways is so difficult for some of our friends who have autism, and why they get so upset if someone bumps into them.

√ Unexpected touch for people with autism can be very disturbing to them and even frightening.

√ Sometimes, too many people too close can feel like touching and not be comfortable for a person with autism.

Activity #6d: Noticing Smells

"He appeared to have an overwhelming physical revulsion to most foods, especially to anything that was a mixture of ingredients." (Barron & Barron 1992, 95)

NOTICING SMELLS

Setting it up:

Again, invite those who choose to participate. Be sure with this activity, as with any of the activities involving latex balloons, to inquire first as to whether there is anyone in the group who might be allergic. If there are, allow those people to leave and try to restrict this activity to an area of the room that will be easily cleared of the scents soon after the completion of the activity. Be sure to include a variety of scents, some of which most people usually find pleasurable (e.g., vanilla) and some that most people don't like (e.g., citronella).

Begin by going around with scented candles in bags or incense in its package, and having the students notice the smells. Then open the candles or incense and light them, again, passing through the classroom and having children smell them all again. Have them notice the difference between smelling the candles or incense in the package and when lit. Have them notice the preferences they experienced around the different smells.

You will need:

A variety of different scented candles and/or incense, and/or aromatherapy oils.

Major points to make:

√ Talk about how typical smells can be intense and/or obnoxious for kids with autism; they might react to a person's perfume, the cooking smells of food from the cafeteria, the smell of Play-Doh, of markers, etc.

√ For some people with autism, their intense sensitivity to different smells makes it very difficult for them to pay attention or talk to you.

√ For some, it makes it difficult for them even to stay in the room. (Remember, they might not be able to tell you why they're leaving.)

√ Some might get severe headaches that they are then unable to tell us about.

√ Some can smell things that you and I don't even notice.

√ Some people really like being able to smell things and get really stuck smelling when they find something that smells good to them.

√ Some people like smelling things or other people because it gives them reliable information, and they don't realize that it isn't something we usually do.

Activity #6e: Visual Distractions

"Distractions in the room may cause me to lose my concentration. If you do need to leave the room during the hour, I probably will stop talking and follow you with my eyes for a moment or two. This is not to embarrass you in any way. Feel free to leave if you have to. I understand that many times at a conference like this, circumstances may require that you leave. I will try not to let it distract me, or to take it personally."

(Ruth Elaine Hane in Gillingham and McClennen 2003, 3)

Setting it up:

Have the students generate a short sentence to be written on the board. As you write it, create a blank space big enough to insert another word between each word of the sentence (e.g., We _____ saw _____ the _____ pigs _____ flying _____ to _____ the _____ moon). Then ask one of two different students to take turns reading the sentence as they created it. Have them notice how easy it was to do that. Next ask one of them to do it again, only this time, every time they get to a blank, ask them to look around the room, notice something with their eyes, and label it out loud. As they label it, insert that label into the appropriate blank.

Read it back to them with the new words inserted in the blanks. Have them talk about how hard it was for them to concentrate when they had to keep noticing things they saw. Have the students who were listening notice how much more difficult it was to understand the person reading.

You will need:

Something upon which to write a sentence that all the students will be able to see.

Major points to make:

√ For some individuals with autism, their eyes are so busy that it is difficult for them to NOT pay attention to what they see, just as we were asking your eyes to stay busy even while you were trying to read the sentence.

√ For some, these "busy eyes" make it seem like they are not paying attention to you or to the teacher or to the activity they are supposed to be doing. Some can't, but some learn to pay attention to both VERY WELL.

√ It is also hard for some people with autism NOT to talk about what they notice. This can sometimes make it difficult to have a conversation, in the same way it was more difficult to understand the sentence being read the second time.

Activity #6f: Sensory Bombardment

"Various stimuli, insignificant to most people, created a full blown stress reaction in me. When the telephone rang or when I checked the mail, I'd have a 'stage fright' nerve attack. What if I didn't get any mail—or what if I did—and it was something bad? The ring of the telephone set off the same reaction—panic. Going bowling in the evening made me nervous and I dreaded the school trips. I was afraid I'd be seized by a panic attack in a public place and wouldn't be able to stand it."

(Grandin & Scariano 1986, 68-69)

"The clamor of many voices, the different smells, perfume, cigars, damp wool caps or gloves—people moving about at different speeds, going in different directions, the constant noise and confusion, the constant touching, were overwhelming."

(Grandin & Scariano 1986, 21)

"But, as a child, since I had no magical, comfort device, I wrapped myself in a blanket or got under sofa cushions to satisfy my desire for tactile stimulation. At night I tucked in the sheets and blankets tightly and then slid under them. Sometimes I wore cardboard posters like a sandwich board man because I enjoyed the pressure of the boards against my body."

(Grandin & Scariano 1986, 29)

Setting it up:

Ask the group to think about an experience that is very relaxing and pleasant to them. Ask them to try to imagine as clearly as they can as many details about that experience as possible. Explain that you would like them to spend some time drawing, writing, or just thinking about that happy, relaxing place. Encourage those who choose to just think about it to close their eyes if they are comfortable enough to do so. Give the group about two minutes to engage in this part of the activity.

Bring them back to the present space and moment. Ask those who were writing/drawing to move their pens or pencils to their non-dominant hand, and ask those who were imagining/visualizing to stand up and face the back of the room. Give them about thirty seconds to return to that happy, relaxing place.

Then, with the help of an assistant, begin playing very loud static or high energy music while your partner flashes the lights on and off. At the same time, begin throwing soft animals/balls and small pieces of candy at the group. Walk through the group with a piece of ribbon or long feather boa, circling it around people's heads or drawing it across their faces and/or arms. Poke and tickle some of the group. Periodically blow a loud whistle or other kind of noise-maker. Encourage them to continue to write or draw or think about their happy, calm place. Do this for about two minutes.

When this bombardment ends, give the group a few seconds to resettle themselves, then begin the discussion of what this experience was like for them. Focus on the feelings they were having as well as their ability to maintain their focus and performance of the task.

You will need:

Something upon which to play loud music or with which to create loud static (one of our colleagues used a taped recording of a fourth grade classroom). Materials for drawing and writing. Small, soft animals and/or balls. Small pieces of candy. A long ribbon or feather boa. A loud whistle or other kind of noisemaker.

Major points to make:

√ This is similar to how many people with autism describe what it is like to be in any kind of group situation.

√ People with autism can not always predict how their sensory system is going to react any more than the people in the group could predict what they were going to experience next during this activity.

√ People with autism react as differently as people in the group did to situations in which they are feeling "bombarded." Some are frightened, some are anxious, some are angry, and some tune out of the group.

√ It often doesn't take as much as it did here to make a person with autism feel this level of sensory bombardment.

√ When people are feeling this bombardment, it is difficult to stay calm and/or feel good.

√ When people are feeling this level of bombardment it is sometimes difficult for them to continue performing the way they could before. Their pictures are not as clear, they can't find words as easily, and they may even forget how to spell words that were simple for them when they were calm and focused. Many of our friends with autism face this kind of challenge every day.

√ Knowing what you are supposed to be doing doesn't really help if you are feeling bombarded.

√ Some people who feel bombarded just quit even trying to participate in the activity. Sometimes that is what our friends with autism have to do as well.

Supplement each of their experiences with a story about either the peer they know or other individuals with autism.

Activity #7: Senses, including Proprioceptive and Vestibular

"They asked him to point at his body parts, but the boy could not do it. Not that he was ignorant of the parts of the human body, but he was unable to point and identify them in his own self. Pointing at objects was difficult too, as he pointed only at the letters on the board and could not generalize it with the other things. Then the doctors asked the other way around. They touched his legs and hands and so on. They asked him to point on the board. This he did with ease."
(Mukhopadhyay 2000, 26)

"I always needed to be on the move. Even when I was made to sit still on a chair, I had to rock it. If I sat on the floor, I needed to rock myself and suck the roof of my mouth—the rhythm and the movement meant I was alive and kept the music going. I think I believed that if I ended the movement, then that would be the end of me."
(Lawson 1998, 24)

Note: It is suggested that an occupational or physical therapist who is trained in sensory integration/sensory processing assist or consult with the presentation of this activity.

Description:

This activity is designed to provide students/staff with an expanded understanding of sensory processing. It works well in conjunction with or as a follow-up to Activity #6, "The Sensory Experience of Autism." After each of the five senses are described and experienced, the students/staff will learn the words "proprioceptive" and "vestibular"; where they are located in the body; and have a chance to experience these two sensory processing systems.

Setting it up:

The teacher/facilitator may want to use a review of Activity # 6 as an introduction to Activity #7. Have the students generate their five senses and where these senses are located in their body. For example:

Sense:	Located in:
sight	eyes
taste	mouth
hearing	ears
smell	nose
touch	skin

Next, write down "Vestibular (which is located in) the inner ear" and "Proprioceptive (which is located in) the joints/muscles" and tell the students/staff they are going to experience these two sensory systems at work.

To experience the vestibular system at work, have the students stand, close their eyes and take a step first to the right, then to the back, then to the left, and finally to the front. This should bring them back to the spot in which they started. Have them open their eyes and discuss how they could ambulate from one place to another without the use of their eyes (i.e., their vestibular system gave them information about where their body was while in movement and thus they could follow the directions without looking).

To experience the proprioceptive system at work, have the students stand and extend their arms parallel to the ground and hold them there. Chat with them, encouraging them to keep their arms up until you tell them to put them down. Have them notice gravity pushing down on their arms (this is their proprioceptive system doing its job!), and what message their proprioceptive system is giving them. It may be saying, "Put your arms down!" Encourage them to keep their arms up just a little longer so that they can remember this experience when they think of the word "proprioceptive." Finally, tell them to put their arms down and sit back in the chairs/desks for the discussion.

You will need:

All that is necessary for this activity is enough space for the students to move around. It is best to conduct the discussions with them in a sitting position, so it is suggested that the teacher/facilitator invite the students/staff to sit down after each of the experiential activities. It is also helpful to have a wall chart, overhead projector and screen, or chalkboard available to write down the words for each of the senses and where they are located in the body (i.e., both the review of the five senses, as well as proprioceptive and vestibular).

Major points to make:

The teacher/facilitator is encouraged, in this activity, to assist the students in extrapolating what it might be like if their vestibular or proprioceptive system didn't work:

√ What things might be difficult for you to do?

√ What might we see from you?

√ Can you think of things that your friend/classmate with autism does that we might theorize is due to difficulties modulating his/her vestibular or proprioceptive system?

√ The teacher/facilitator might also want to discuss what kinds of strategies are used with the student with autism to assist him/her in modulating his/her system.

The "Engines Program" or "Alert Program," which comes out of the work of Williams and Shellenberger (1994), is a nice adjunct to any discussion or sensitivity training on sensory processing in students with autism. This program teaches students to read their own sensory systems in a nonjudgmental manner, to determine if their sensory "engine" is running too high, just right, or too low. The emphasis is on the students learning what kinds of input alerts and calms them and applying it differentially depending on how their engine is running. This teaching can be used as a sensitivity training in and of itself, to illustrate the difference in all our sensory systems, as well as the natural fluctuations in sensory systems. It can be fun for peers to take some time to notice and learn about their own sensory preferences and styles, and then contrast them with each other and their classmate with autism.

One other hands-on activity that can be used in any classroom situation or sensitivity training is the use of "fiddle baskets" or "bins." These are containers filled with all sorts of sensory-based toys that can be purchased at any local toy store. Examples of items that might be in a sensory fiddle basket: koosh balls; balloons filled with sand or rice; sparkle sticks; water bottle; water toys; mechanical toys that spin; smooth stones; kaleidoscopes; tops; small vibrating toys; things to chew; aroma-based and scented items; squeeze balls; weighted animals; etc.

If a fiddle basket is available to students while instruction is occurring, they will have an opportunity to notice which type of sensory input makes it easier for them to process information coming in; they may notice that they prefer a different fiddle object when they are processing auditory information than when they are doing work independently. Or, they may notice that they aren't drawn to use any fiddle toy. All of the information they learn about themselves can eventually be tied back into discussions about their classmate with autism and his/her varying sensory needs.

[Portions of this activity were inspired by presentations given by Patty Mader-Ebert and Deborah Kowalkowski-Funk.]

Activity #8: Neuropathways

"I believe that autism results when some sort of mechanism that controls emotion does not functions properly, leaving an otherwise relatively normal body and mind unable to express themselves with the depth that they would otherwise be capable of."
(Williams 1992, 203)

"My brain was like a department store where the people running different departments were working alternate shifts. When one came to work, the others went to sleep—background, foreground. Lucky for me I could sleep-walk and sleep-talk."
(Williams 1994, 96)

Description:

It has been noted repeatedly in the literature and research on autism that most people with this disability have a strength in learning through visually supported information (Grandin 1988; Hodgdon 1995; Hurlburt, Happe and Frith 1994). Many individuals with autism perform better and feel more comfortable within the context of predictable routines and familiarity. This activity is designed to teach these characteristics in an experiential manner, as well as demonstrate that, to a certain extent, the same holds true for all of us. The students will be set up as neuropathways passing information. The neuropathways will be passing the following information:

Neuropathway #1: *Physical Complex.* Unfamiliar, long physical input with no rhythm (i.e., push, pull, and tap on the person with no real pattern or rhythm).

Neuropathway #2: *Physical Simple.* Short physical input with rhythm (e.g., two short pushes on the shoulders followed by shaking the hand three times).

Neuropathway #3: *Verbal Familiar* (e.g., "Mary had a little lamb").

Neuropathway #4: *Verbal Unfamiliar* (nonsense syllables) without a rhythm (e.g., "snickle boola dada").

Neuropathway #5: *Verbal Unfamiliar* (nonsense syllables) with a rhythm and repetition (e.g., "dee dee dee da da da moo moo moo").

Neuropathway #6: *Visual Familiar* (e.g., a piece of paper with the phrase "Mary had a little lamb" written on it).

Neuropathway #7: *Visual Unfamiliar* (e.g., a piece of paper with "snickle boola dada" written on it).

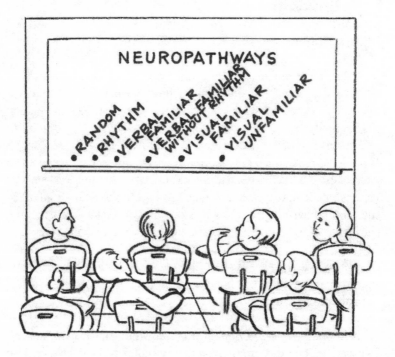

Setting it up:

The teacher/facilitator has students place their chairs in seven rows. Each row represents one neuropathway. It doesn't matter how many students are in each row, although it works best with at least five students per row. If necessary, there can be more than seven rows, in which case the teacher/facilitator would simply repeat the type of input given to neuropathway #1, #2, and so on.

Tell the students that they are going to play a game that is similar to a game with which they may be familiar: "telephone." Explain to them that you are going to give a message to the person sitting in the first chair of each row and they are going to "pretend to be a brain" by passing the information to the next person. Explain that some "neuropathways" (use the term "parts of the brain" for younger students) will need to transmit verbal information, while others will be passing tactile or physical and still others will be passing visual or written information. (Note: Check which students/staff prefer NOT to be touched and suggest they join rows #3 - #7.)

When providing the input to the first person in rows #1 and #2, ask the other people in the respective row to look away (so that the information can remain solely physical and not visual, as if they see it).

You will need:

All the teacher/facilitator will need is a group of students or staff and chairs that can easily be moved into rows, and small pieces of paper and writing utensils. It is also helpful to have a wall chart or chalkboard on which to write the types of neuropathways (without the examples).

Major points to make:

After all the pathways are finished passing their information, check with the last person in each row as to what they "received." Chances are that the complex physical will not have gotten through accurately, while the simple physical with a rhythm will have. Use the first two neuropathways to make at least the following points:

√ You will likely find that row #1 may not be finished when even row #7 is completed. This will assist in making the point that complex physical information is one of the most difficult to pass through the cognitive neuropathway. The person at the end of row #1 may say something to the effect of, "I don't know what s/he did to me, I only know it felt good." That is because the system may not code all the specifics of physical input, particularly when it is complex and disorganized.

√ Assist students in applying this new knowledge to the student they may know with autism, in terms of what types of tasks this may indicate would be difficult for their classmate with autism (e.g., some sports, some daily living skills), as well as how they might approach the classmate with autism differently, with this new knowledge in hand.

√ Assist students in noticing that once the physical input was simple and rhythmic, as in row #2, the information passed much more quickly and accurately. This is also true for students with autism, and highlights for us why some physical prompting, if done well, can be instrumental in their learning.

Next, check in with the last person in rows #3, #4, and #5 to see what information was passed, how quickly and how accurately. What usually happens here is that #5 is nowhere in the ballpark of what the initial input was. In #4, it is often the case that the rhythm of the "dee dee dee da da da ... " got through in some manner. And, in #3, of course, it almost always gets through because it is familiar. Again, use this check-in with the person at the end of each row to illustrate the following points:

√ Verbal information that is novel is more difficult to pass through the brain than verbal information that is familiar.

√ Verbal information that has a pattern or a rhythm (as in the "dee dee dee da da da ... ") may pass through more easily, even if it is unfamiliar.

√ Familiar verbal information passes through accurately and quickly.

Finally, check in with the last person in rows #6 and #7. What will be true is that, since they were simply passing a slip of paper with first a familiar phrase written on it (#6) and then an unfamiliar phrase written on it (#7), the messages will have gotten through quickly and accurately. The point to make here is:

√ Visual information is the fastest to process and understand, even when it is unfamiliar.

This can launch a discussion of what the most useful type of interaction might be for their classmate with autism. Especially with older students, it can be useful to ask those who have successful relationships with the individual with autism to describe their interactive style and how/what they might already be doing that fits well into their classmate's processing style.

[Portions of this activity and the next were inspired by a presentation given by Jane Webfer, OTR, and Susan Vaughan Kratz, OTR, BCP.]

Activity #9: Monochannel Functioning & Balloons

"People who work in 'mono' are like the trains rather than the network. They are this train or that train or the other train but they generally aren't all the trains all at once. For these people to process what they are watching whilst walking may mean that their body seems to arrive at places as if by magic. To process the meaning of what they are listening to whilst being touched may be to have no idea where they were being touched or what they thought or felt about it. To process the location or social significance of being touched whilst someone is showing them something may mean that they saw nothing but meaningless color and form and movement."
(Williams 1996, 96)

"I knew that my sense worked in mono and that my limbs did, too. I knew that comprehension and expression worked in mono and so did sense of self and other. I knew that feelings and thought and words and pictures often worked in mono, but because I had always used my eyes to scan rather than look, I hadn't known that my eyes could work in mono as separate organs rather than in stereo. I set about becoming aware when an eye stopped registering and which one it was. Then I'd focus my abilities on using that one and hope it wouldn't be at the expense of the other one. If the other one switched off mentally, I focused on that one, until I could switch from one to the other at will. I would take control of these difficulties. They would not control me. They would not dictate my reality, nor have me walk into walls and doorways and think myself clumsy."
(Williams 1996, 110)

Description:

When Donna Williams, a renowned person with autism, presented a keynote address at a national conference on autism in 1995, she provided some critical and insightful information about the difficulties people with autism may experience in processing sensory information (Kurtz 1995). While Donna acknowledged that all people with the label of autism experience the condition differently, she explained that for her, autism is a problem of information overload. This overload occurs when information is coming in too quickly for her to process it or when she is neurologically unable to filter out irrelevant stimuli.

In her keynote, Donna compared her sensory system to a soundtrack. She articulated how, while most of us can process information on several tracks at once in a "multi-track" mode, she often processes in a "mono-track" mode. For her, systems shift and shut down. One system of sensory processing may come when another goes. Donna perceives this shifting and shutting down of sensory systems as an involuntary compensation for information overload.

It is believed that this shifting and shutting down is a phenomenon that many people with autism may experience. If one reflects on the impact this particular sensory processing difficulty may have on the experience of the world for individuals with autism, it becomes apparent that, in order to have relationship with someone with autism, it is necessary to understand what this experience represents and feels like for them.

The following activity was designed to give students an understanding of this particular sensory processing difficulty that many people with autism experience. The activity entails first having everyone keep balloons in the air, with different body parts representing each sensory system. (Note: It may be helpful to do Activity #6 and Activity #7 to provide information on sensory systems, if students aren't familiar with them.) The teacher/facilitator explains that we are going to play a game where certain body parts represent certain sensory systems (i.e., hearing, sight, touch, taste, smell):

Right Hand represents hearing.
Left Hand represents touch.
Left Leg represents taste.
Right Leg represents smell.
Eyes represent sight.

The activity starts with the students each blowing up and tying a balloon. Next, the teacher/facilitator has them play a game of trying to keep the balloons in the air. Tell them they can use all parts of their bodies; all their "sensory systems." Once a balloon touches the ground, it is out of play until the next round. When all of the balloons have grounded, the teacher/facilitator praises the students for how well they did "their work" of keeping the balloons in the air.

Next, the teacher/facilitator explains that for the next round, one "sensory system" will shut down on them. S/he explains that now, they will not be able to use one of their sensory systems, represented by their dominant hand. Thus, the students play the next round with their dominant hand behind their backs.

Round three, have the students stand on one leg, taking out another sensory system.

Round four, take out the other leg, requiring them to sit down, only able to use their non-dominant hand.

Next, take out their sight by having them close their eyes, and using only their non-dominant hands.

Note: It may be useful for younger students to have the names of the five senses taped on each representing body part, to clarify the symbolic reference.

Setting it up:

Teacher/facilitator leads a discussion with the students about sensory systems and what they do for us. Then, talk about how this may happen differently for their friend/classmate with autism. Depending on the age of the students, it may be helpful to discuss the process of shifts and shutdowns. Next, explain the activity and the body parts representing different sensory systems.

You will need:

Balloons. It is best to have one per student or at least one for every other student. (Caution: Find out ahead of time if any of the students have a latex allergy or sensitivity and what the extent of their allergy/sensitivity may be. Sometimes, the person can observe the activity from the hallway and still participate in follow-up discussions. Sometimes, the person can participate as long as the balloons are collected and removed from the room immediately following the activity.)

To enhance the experience of feeling pressured to perform, the teacher/facilitator may want to provide prizes for the person/people who keep a balloon in the air the longest.

Major points to make:

√ Ask the students what it felt like to know they could keep the balloons afloat with all their body parts or "senses" and then to have the teacher/facilitator arbitrarily cut some of their abilities off. Help the students make the connection between their experience with the balloons and that of their friend/classmate with autism. For example, a person with autism may have difficulty with group discussions. If s/he is in overload and has switched to only being able to see, that would make it impossible to process and participate verbally.

√ We all experience the world differently. Your friend/classmate with autism may not consistently be able to feel your touch or understand what you are saying. Later, those abilities may come back. Think about how that would feel to you.

√ Talk about what would have been helpful when they couldn't "access all their skills."

√ Depending on the age and sensitivity of the students, the teacher/facilitator may want to give differential feedback to the students based on their performance. Without embarrassing the students, the teacher may make comments like, "Come on, I know you can do this!"; or, "What's wrong with you? You were just keeping those balloons in the air and now they're falling all over the place!" This replicates the experience that many people with autism may have around not being able to access their senses and, consequently, information or movement, and having people in the environment become angry or frustrated while they are experiencing a processing deficit.

Activity #10: Exclusion/Privilege Experience

"I had a driving need to ask questions about the states because I felt I could not talk the way 'normal' people talked, nor could I take part in their conversations, since I didn't understand them. Everyone else talked effortlessly, their conversations flowing as smoothly as a creek, and I felt very inferior, shut out, less important ... Even if I couldn't talk the way everyone else did, I could dominate and control what was said ... I wanted to get attention for something other than the things I did that were wrong! ... At the time however, what mattered was that doing it made me feel a little closer to being a normal human being."

(Barron & Barron 1992, 105)

"I realize there are times I don't want to go off with groups from my class but I think part of this attitude is fear. Another part is defensiveness because I don't want to be with them. They do like me and when they see me outside (when I happen to drift past people in my class) they call me over. I understand that and I join them but I am finding myself increasingly left out and I am sure they think this is my choice (which is only half true). This makes it even harder for me ... Once I sit with them, sometimes I can talk well but because I don't follow their topics I either am quiet or I direct people's cues to talk (nicely, but I know this is not what others do), and still I can't work out what they do do. They have no system (unlike in class). I guess that is language, but socially I have a lot of problems with this when it is not coming from me."

(Williams 1994, 78)

Description:

Life continually presents us with situations in which we feel included or excluded. Individuals with autism may chronically feel excluded. The following activity gives peers a chance to notice the feelings of being both included/privileged or excluded.

The teacher/facilitator has the children generate a list of five to six arbitrary letters of the alphabet and writes those letters on the chalkboard. S/he asks the children whose names begin with these letters to form a group in one corner or area of the classroom. Next, the teacher/facilitator invites all the other children to choose a game they would like to play and passes out a small treat to these children, thereby excluding those gathered in the corner of the room.

Play the game for one or two rounds, ignoring comments that might be made by those in the corner or reminding the "corner group" that they aren't really a part of this. Call time to the game and apologize to the excluded group and thank them for participating, explaining that the purpose of this activity was for them to experience the emotional effects of having been excluded. Have the children engage in some re-joining gesture (bow of peace; peace push [see page 100]; handshakes), including having one of the privileged children offer the treats to the excluded group. Conclude by facilitating a discussion around what it felt like for each group, whether they were excluded or privileged.

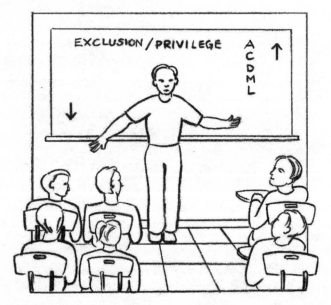

Setting it up:

Explain to the children that we all have different life experiences in which we are sometimes in the group or out of the group. We are going to try one of those experiences now.

You will need:

A snack and an idea for a game in the event the children don't come up with one.

Examples for younger children: Simon Says; Hang Man; I Spy; Twenty Questions.

Examples for older children: Password; Seven Up; Hang Man; Twenty Questions; Charades.

Major points to make:

√ In many life experiences, some people end up feeling privileged and others, excluded. Reflect and validate the children's feelings from each of the groups. It may be helpful to write these in columns as the children are generating them.

√ For some people, their exclusion feels as arbitrary as what letter their last name begins with (e.g., someone who doesn't walk as well; think in the same manner; communicate as easily). Have them generate when this might happen for the students with autism they know. Tie this into the student(s) with autism.

√ Reflect with the children what it was like when they invited the excluded group back in. Address the fact that some of the privileged children may have felt power and didn't want to invite the other children back in. Others, from the privileged group, may have felt compassion and consequently were relieved to invite the others back in. And, some of the children may have had mixed feelings, or even guilt.

Activity #11: Social Barriers

"I had no idea how to make friends or to fit in with other kids at school. There was a new sophistication in the way they teased me ... name-calling turned to practical jokes. The worse thing was never knowing whom I could trust or when I could trust them. I know now that the way I behaved made everything worse, but I didn't know at the time, and I couldn't help it."
(Barron & Barron 1992, 179)

Description:

Many children experience being outside of a social barrier at some point in their lives. Garrity et al. (1996) has developed an entire curriculum to assist schools and families in "bully proofing" environments. Additionally, Peter Yarrow (of Peter, Paul and Mary) has helped to develop a similar curriculum called "Don't Laugh at Me" that is designed to address bullying in general (see Existing Resources in the Appendix, page 143). The next activity is designed to assist students to directly experience the feelings of being "bullied" or acting the "bully" (in a safe, adult-facilitated situation).

This activity usually works best if it follows Activity #10, Exclusion/Privilege. The teacher begins by having the students generate hurtful words that they have heard others saying to their peer with autism, to other classmates, or to themselves. (Note: It is important to set a boundary that we are going to avoid words that are pejorative re: race, gender, and sexual orientation.) The teacher/facilitator writes these words on the board. Next, the teacher/facilitator invites the students who had been in the privilege group in Activity #10 to stand together in the middle of the room. Instruct all students that when the activity begins they will be using words only, being sure to keep their hands and bodies to themselves. Then, s/he takes the other students in the hallway and explains that when s/he says 'go' they are to get in the face of the students in the room's center and yell the hurtful words at them. When s/he says "stop" they are to stop. The facilitator uses his/her judgment in regards to the length of time spent yelling. It should not exceed one minute, and might need to be shorter.

Setting it up:

It will be important to explain to the students that they will be playacting and that it is useful for them to notice their feelings as the activity progresses. (Note: This activity is best suited for upper elementary, middle and high school students. Younger children may not be capable of shifting in and out of the role playing in a manner which allows them to experience the activity without sustained emotional difficulty.)

After the teacher/facilitator has directed the name-callers to "stop," it is best to have the two groups interact in a manner that allows them to shift positively out of their assigned roles and back into compatible classmates. Some ways to accomplish this are:

1. Shake one another's hands as a sign of kind reconnection.

2. Do some group "peace breathing" (take a deep breath in, then on the out breath slowly say, "peeeeeaaaaaaaccccccccc-ccceeeee").

3. Have the students pair up with a student from the other group, take a deep cleansing breath together, making eye contact and smiling.

4. Have the students pair up with a student from the other group and do the "peace push" together (i.e., stand facing each other, hold bent arms up such that palms are facing out; lean body weight to push against the other person's hands with just the right amount of force such that the pair stays in balance).

Conclude the activity by having the bullying group pass out treats to the bullied group.

You will need:

A large enough room for students to occupy the center and still have space around them for other students to move.

A board on which to write (chalkboard, dry erase board) generated hurtful words.

Treats.

Major points to make:

√ Process what it felt like for the group in the center to be bullied/have hurtful words yelled at them. What thoughts went through their heads? What did they think of doing?

√ Process what it felt like for the other group to be doing the name calling. Interestingly, many of the children feel quite uncomfortable in this role, perhaps as uncomfortable as the others feel being called names.

√ Talk about what it would feel like not to be able to talk or access your words reliably, such as a student with autism, and have someone calling you names.

√ Talk about what it would feel like not to be able to remove yourself from a situation where you are being teased, bullied, harassed, such as what might happen for them or their classmate with autism.

Note: It is important to check in with the students to make certain they have shifted out of the playacting. If a student(s) has been unable to leave the role behind, find out if s/he knows what s/he needs to do so and even engage other students in this process of problem solving.

Activity #12: Helping

"I know that I should say, 'Goodbye!' to the speaker after these one-sided conversations, but cannot spontaneously look at someone and speak. Instead I glance sideways and walk off, or wait for someone else to tell me that this is the moment to say farewell. Then I flap my hand in a vestige of the wave that my sisters instilled in me with so much effort, and mutter, 'Bye bye,' as woodenly as twenty years ago, my eyes often flashing back to the person who has reminded me of what to say, and on whom I am relying for timing and reinforcement."

(Blackman 1999, 42)

Description:

The teacher/facilitator begins by introducing and reviewing the cycle of help:

"We all begin life as babies. Think about how much help babies need. In the beginning they need bigger people to do almost everything for them. Then, as we grow, we need less help. We grow and learn how to do more and more for ourselves, moving closer and closer toward independence. Then as we grow older and older, or if something happens to us, we find we begin to need more help again.

"Help is a funny thing. Sometimes we are lucky, and we get just the amount of help we need. Sometimes we want help, but don't get it for some reason. Sometimes we get too much help. Let's play a little with how it feels to give and get different kinds and amounts of help."

First, the participants are divided into two groups: those who will be helpers, and those who will experience a challenge. The latter group is then divided into three subgroups:

1. Participants who will experience a vision impairment. (Have the individuals wear pairs of sunglasses that have lenses smeared with vaseline.)

2. Participants who will experience a hearing impairment. (Have the individuals wear earplugs or cotton balls in their ears.)

3. Participants who will experience a physical challenge. (Have the individuals wear a mitten on their non-dominant hand, and instruct them to use that hand only.)

Assign each participant one "helper." Helpers will be given directions to provide either too much, too little, or "just the right amount" of help.

Set "learners" up with their experiences and their activities.

Some suggested activities:

• For the learner experiencing a vision impairment: a lotto, a puzzle or anything else that requires good vision.

• For the learner experiencing a hearing impairment: a spelling test, an oral quiz on a familiar topic, or anything else that requires good hearing/auditory processing.

• For the learner experiencing the physical challenge: a stacking activity, a lotto, a puzzle, or anything else that requires good motor control.

Take "helpers" out to review their scripts (see page 105).

Bring the group together. Have learners begin their activities and helpers follow their scripts. Allow interactions to go on for about 2-3 minutes.

Following the experience, have those who were helped share their feelings. Then ask the helpers to talk about their experience. Next, move into a discussion about how people who frequently and regularly need help have experienced all of those feelings and probably do every day. Try to get examples from them of when some of these times might be.

Setting it up:

Tell students/staff that throughout our lives there are times we all need a little bit of help from one another. Let them know that this activity will give them a chance to explore some issues that often arise around when we help each other and the kind of help we give one another.

You will need:

Sunglasses with lenses smeared with vaseline (to create a vision impairment).

Ear plugs/cotton balls to create a hearing impairment.

Mittens to create a motor challenge.

Puzzles with thin pieces.

Lotto board.

Paper and pen/crayons/markers.

Stacking activity.

"Helpers' Scripts." You can print these scripts and pass them out, or give the directions verbally to each group of "helpers":

Script for Helpers Group #1:

MAKE SURE THIS TASK GETS DONE, EVEN IF YOU HAVE TO DO ALL OF IT FOR THE PERSON. DO NOT LET THIS PERSON MAKE ANY MISTAKES. IF S/HE STARTS TO MAKE A MISTAKE; YOU DO IT FOR HIM/HER. CONTINUE TO REMIND HIM/HER THAT YOU ARE THERE TO HELP THEM, AND THAT YOU WILL DO IT FOR THEM IF THEY NEED YOU TO DO SO ... AND THEN DO SO!

Script for Helpers Group #2:

DO NOT DO ANY OF THIS TASK FOR THE PERSON. IF S/HE IS HAVING A HARD TIME, JUST TELL THEM THAT THEY CAN GET IT AND TO KEEP TRYING. JUST GIVE HIM/HER WORDS AS HELP.

Script for Helpers Group #3:

GIVE THIS PERSON AS MUCH HELP AS S/HE RE-QUESTS. ENCOURAGE THEM TO TRY ON THEIR OWN, BUT IF YOU CAN FIGURE OUT A WAY TO DO IT TOGETHER THAT IS FINE. CONTINUE TO MAKE SURE YOU ARE GIV-ING THE AMOUNT OF HELP S/HE WANTS AND MAKE SURE YOU ARE HELPING IN THE WAY THEY WANT.

Major points to make:

√ Getting help when you haven't asked for it can feel … irritating, humiliating, annoying, etc. When you feel this way you might get angry or you might just give up all together and quit trying at all.

√ Getting just the right amount of help can feel very supportive and good.

√ Getting help when you ask for it can feel very supportive and good.

√ Not getting help when you have asked for it or clearly need it can feel very frustrating. As a result, you might get angry, or you might just give up and not try anymore.

√ Talk about the importance of allowing everyone in our lives to do as much as they can on their own, noticing the times they seem to be needing help. When we notice, it is important to let people (peers) ask for help rather than just jumping in with assistance. Our help needs to be their choice. Help needs to be the choice for both people.

3. PULLING IT ALL TOGETHER

Individualizing

As with all kinds of teaching, it is important to individualize your content and presentation when conducting sensitivity training. A part of this decision will be determined by how much time you have in a given situation. The design of the activities discussed in Chapter Two allows long or short discussions; lengthy or brief presentation. Set aside a minimum of twenty or thirty minutes for each activity. All of the activities can certainly go longer than that.

A. Peer Surveys

When individualizing your presentation, it can also be helpful to use peer surveys to guide your decision about which activities to choose.

Following are sample responses to student surveys which were mentioned in Chapter Two (pages 31-32). The student whose peers were surveyed was a ninth grade student and the survey was conducted early in the school year.

Question #1: You have had the opportunity to be with Andrew for about two weeks. What questions do you have about him and/or his abilities? What are you curious about? What would you like to know about Andrew and/or autism?

PHYSICAL EDUCATION

—Is there a cure for autism in the works?

—This has already been explained to me.

—What is autism? What are the effects of autism?

—Is autism hereditary? How many people have autism? Are there still kids in elementary schools?

"FOODS FOR TODAY" CLASS

—Why doesn't he talk? Is he really smart? What does he think about? How is he going to cope when he's older?

—If he does by chance throw a tantrum in class what are we supposed to do?

—If we talk to Andrew and he has a fit, what do we do?

—How did he get autism?

—Is his life cut shorter because of his disease? Was he born with it? How did you know he had the disease? If I want to talk to him, would he talk back to me?

SCIENCE

—Is there a cure for autism?

—Has Andrew had autism his whole life? What are some of Andrew's strengths? How many people have autism in the US? What ways does Andrew communicate with other people?

—What happened to the typewriter he [used to] carry around? Does he know when I say hi to him? How do we learn to accept his behavior?

PHYSICAL EDUCATION

—What's his favorite sport?

—Did he get a grade point average this year? If so, what was it?

—What are his capabilities?

—What kind of autism does he have? What level is his autism at?

—I don't have any questions.

—On the bus he sometimes bursts out laughing. Why does he do this?

—How did Andrew get autism? Will Andrew's autism get better as he gets older?

—Can Andrew get along well with other people with autism?

Question #2: How do other kids treat Andrew in the cafeteria, hallway, classroom, bus, etc.? Are they helpful, nice, kind, mean? Do people just ignore him? Do people seem afraid of him?

PHYSICAL EDUCATION

—Most kids treat him very well. They certainly aren't scared of him.

—I don't ever see him.

—I think people just will look at him, they are very nice. People will sometimes ignore him because most don't know what Andrew has. I don't think people are afraid of Andrew at all.

—People are nice to Andrew. On the bus no one really says much, but some say hello.

—I think that some people are just clueless about what to say. Otherwise Andrew is a cool kid and a lot of people know that. I don't think that people are trying to ignore him. People do not seem afraid of him.

—They are all nice to him.

—From what I see, people are all around nice to him.

—Some ignore him. Others are extremely helpful to him.

—Helpful, nice, scared.

—They are nice to him.

—Helpful, kind, nice.

—Other kids usually seem to try to be nice and kind to Andrew.

—When people see Andrew in the hallway they just ignore him. I knew Andrew in middle school and he always had to leave the room; and now I see him in the hall he can say more than when we were in middle school. When I say hi to Andrew it takes him awhile to get it out, but being with him in middle school I understand why it takes him so long to answer.

—They are always very nice. I've always said hi to him.

"FOODS FOR TODAY" CLASS

—They laugh behind his back. People don't know what to think

—I'm not sure because I don't see him outside of class.

—I think people are kind for the most part, but they ignore him mostly.

—Ignore him.

—Some just ignore him, but some are nice and I haven't seen anyone be mean.

—People treat him nice, but sometimes people are mean to him. Some people don't really talk to Andrew because they are afraid of what Andrew might say or do.

—Give him mean looks sometimes. Some people just ignore him. Also, some people could be very nice to him.

SCIENCE

—They are nice to him.

—Most people ignore him.

—People seem kind to him.

—People that I have seen are very nice to Andrew; everyone understands. People are also helpful and nice. People that don't know him usually just don't do anything mean.

—People are usually nice to him. Sometimes people laugh when he makes noises because they may not know about him. Some people ignore him because they don't know how to act.

—Most people are very kind to him. They always greet him and pat him on the back or something. People are helpful to him, most try to be his friend and understand him more.

—Most freshmen are really nice to him and say hi, but some people who don't know him act weird around him. On our bus, everyone is really quiet. Andrew just sits there along with everyone else.

PHYSICAL EDUCATION

—Kind to him.

—Nice.

—Pretty nice to him, but most people just ignore him because they probably don't know what to say.

—I think many people accept Andrew and are nice to him.

—Nice to him. They don't pay much attention to him.

—Nice.

—I don't see him very much but when I do he doesn't get talked to.

—They talk to him like he is an ordinary person. No one makes fun of him.

—I think people are very nice to him and if they are not, people let them know. I don't think anyone is afraid.

—People are really nice and helpful to Andrew. I don't think anyone is afraid.

—Most people I've seen are pretty nice. Many people do ignore him, but I think it's just because they don't know him.

—A lot of kids that I see are nice to Andrew. I don't think anyone is mean to him. Other people ignore him.

—People that I see say "hi" to Andrew and they treat him nicely. I've never seen or heard anyone be mean to Andrew. I think some people ignore him just so they don't do or say the wrong thing to upset him.

—People are really nice to Andrew for what I see anyways. Everyone talks to him like a normal person. No one seems to be afraid of him.

—No one is afraid of him and I don't really think that people overly pay attention to him. They treat him like a human.

—They help him. People that don't know him, ignore him. In the cafeteria people used to ask him to sit with them (I don't know if they do anymore).

Question #3: What do you think YOU can do to help Andrew be successful for the amount of time he is in your class? (Examples: greet him daily, invite him to join your group, cue him to try to remain with the activity, offer to photocopy your notes for him to study from, etc.)

PHYSICAL EDUCATION

—I could walk around with him. I could treat him as one of my friends as much as possible. I could talk to him more. I could try and help him to understand more that's going on.

—I always say hello to Andrew. Try to help him stay calm on the bus, and at times I just sit with him and chat about his day.

—Treat him like one of us.

—I will try to do everything in my will to make Andrew feel accepted. I will do anything that is needed of me.

—I could say hi to him every day and help him when he is having a hard time with something.

—Talk to him.

—Say hi every day I see him. Be nice to him every day.

—Make him feel welcome in your group. Help him if he is having trouble with a task or something like that. We could try to make him feel important and like we want him to be the best he can be.

—Say hi. Tell him what we are doing.

—Include him on what we are doing. Say hi to him whenever you see him. Don't yell at him, but let him understand that he needs to be quiet and stay with the group.

"FOODS FOR TODAY" CLASS

—Say hi.

—Treat him like I do everyone else.

—Just be kind and get him involved.

—Be friendly.

—Just say hi and be nice to him and help him out if he needs it.

—Treat him like you would treat any other student. Treat him like you would want to be treated.

—Tell people outside of class about his disease and tell them it's not his fault. Try to make him feel comfortable.

SCIENCE

—Say hi to him and acknowledge that he is there.

—Say hi to him.

—Include him in lab.

—I always greet him. I would let him help us in a lab.

—Ask him to work on our lab with me. I would like to learn more about autism and Andrew for a greater understanding.

—I could say hi to him often. I could help him during labs.

—We could request for him to be in our group. I could go out of my way to make sure he is comfortable in his surroundings in class.

PHYSICAL EDUCATION

—Say hi or talk to him.

—Tell him hi; Include him.

—I could greet him when I see him.

—Say hi to him; Talk to him; Play games with him; Give him a high five.

—Say hi to him; Encourage him.

—Say hi to him and generally be nice.

—We could ask if he wanted to join our group in gym. We could teach him something new or how to make something easier.

—Treat him normally like everyone else.

Applying Survey Results

In looking over the answers from the students above, it becomes apparent that the Foods for Today class has a strikingly different perception of how Andrew is treated outside of the class. Therefore, it would be recommended that sensitivity training be done with this class, and the following activities would be suggested:

Activity #1: Visualization.
Activity #6: The Sensory Experience of Autism.
Activity #7: Senses, Including Proprioceptive & Vestibular.
Activity #9: Monochannel Functioning and Balloons.

Perhaps from the sensory activities and visualization, it would be useful to move into some of the inclusion and/or diversity activities to instill a stronger sense of tolerance and acceptance in the Foods for Today class. Of course, it is not necessarily true that just because the students in the Foods for Today class witnessed some mean behavior toward Andrew that they are, in fact, the ones exhibiting it. However, it is the "least dangerous assumption" (Donnellan 1984) to assume that they will benefit from some activities to make sense of what they witnessed and/or participated in.

Also, many of the students had questions about autism's cause and whether or not there is a cure. It may be helpful to find a way via presentation or reading to provide some basic information about autism (see Appendix, pages 145-6).

Tailoring a Presentation

Another dimension in individualizing your presentation is who your audience is and what your situation suggests. Sometimes, it can be helpful to put together a generic overall presentation that you will repeat on a regular basis to a different set of students. This was the case for a creative speech/language therapist named Heidi Martell. She pulled together the following presentation, which she presents at "Diversity Days" at the high school where she works. The students can choose to go to one of many different booths, all designed to educate them on some aspect of diversity. She created her own version of "Planet Autism" for students to visit:

Welcome to Planet Autism

On this planet, we all have some difficulty with differentiating and understanding a variety of sensory input. Sometimes, we don't understand auditory input, other days we have trouble with visual and tactile input. Every day we may have trouble blocking out the smells and sounds that are around us. Some days we have tapes of sound that keep replaying in our head and we cannot do anything to stop the audiotape.

We will give you a short tour of our planet. We will break down all sensory inputs and try to let you see how it feels to enter Planet Autism with only a visitor's visa:

- Audio: Please listen to the audiotape while at the same time writing your name, address, and phone number with your non-dominant hand. (The speech/language therapist has a tape playing with noisy scratching, screaming, and "weird" sounds.)

• Visual: Please look at this drawing and describe what you see:

(If the students say, "It's a duck," she responds: "No! Look again." If they say "Bunny," she says: "No, look again!" Then the therapist uses the experience to teach the students what it feels like when you look at something, think you know what it is and then are told, "NO!")

• Tactile: Try to pick up these pins while wearing a glove on your hand. Was your ability to pick up the pins hampered by your decreased tactile skills? What if you were hyper-sensitive to touch and it hurt to touch or to be touched? What types of activities would you avoid?

• Taste: Want to taste these beans? They're really good, or they may be a strange flavor. (She uses Bernie Botts beans from the *Harry Potter* series, which include the "flavors" vomit, dirt, grass, and ear wax.) You never really know what you're going to find on Planet Autism. You better not try new things. Stick with the same old foods that you can trust. I dare you to try "vomit"!

• Smell: This is how perfume smells on Planet Autism. Please don't wear any or I won't be able to concentrate all day. (The "perfume" is vinegar in a pretty bottle. She uses this to launch a discussion on differences in the olfactory systems of some individuals with autism.)

The demonstration concludes by inviting students to contact the speech/language therapist if they are interested in learning more about individuals with autism or being part of a friendship group with a peer with autism.

Community Outreach

Sometimes, we may be asked to reach beyond the school to share our perspective and understanding about autism.

Consider this scenario: A young adult with autism receives some of his school programming in the community. He has IEP goals, objectives, and benchmarks which address teaching him pedestrian safety, purchasing in natural environments, and vocational skills. On one of his regularly scheduled times in the community, he becomes agitated, biting his hand. In an attempt to stop him from hurting himself and to address some of the student's known sensory needs, the staff person provides deep pressure via a bear hug. However, they both lose their balance and end up on the ground. A concerned passerby calls the police, who arrive and question the staff person.

This true story reminds us that sometimes people other than families, staff and peers need information that will assist them in better serving and interacting with individuals with autism.

Following are some strategies and materials for providing sensitivity training outside of the school setting.

A. Community Card

There are times when individuals with autism may be in public settings either by themselves or with friends, family or support persons. Curious and caring strangers may ask questions, offer assistance or attempt to interact either with the individual or someone in their company. There are many times that these well-meaning attempts can feel/be intrusive or even disruptive.

While it is tempting to ignore or make a curt remark to others in these situations, they can also be used as further opportunities for educating and sensitizing the greater community. One strategy for addressing this opportunity in a manner that is respectful to the individual with autism and the Good Samaritan is to have a small business-sized card printed up that be easily handed to someone without having to engage in conversation. The card might have some very general points about autism, a phone number or website where the stranger can obtain further information, and whatever other information the individual with autism and his/her family is comfortable sharing.

Following is an example of a card that Matt Ward carries with him and hands to people with whom he needs to interact or who ask questions of him. In some cases, it will be necessary for a support person or family member to carry the card; in other cases, the person with autism is capable of doing so him/herself.

> My name is Matt Ward. I have autism. I am smart but I have difficulty with conversation. I understand most things people tell me. Please give me extra time to answer your questions.
>
> If you need more information, contact my parents (named them) at (home and work numbers).

B. EMT Presentation

One school district was asked to give a presentation on autism to the local EMT (Emergency Medical Team). This is a portion of that presentation, given by Sarah Pedersen and Sharon Smith, which could be adapted/used for similar requests which might be made of the reader.

Ways to help kids with autism in a crisis

During times of high stress, kids with autism may demonstrate:

• Excessive laughing or crying.

• Strange sounds, screaming, yelling, and howling.

• Repetitive language.

• Excessive responses to stimuli; covering ears or eyes.

• Self stimulatory behavior or "stimming"—many forms; might be with hands, objects, making sounds, etc.

• Seek sensory input; might include head banging, spinning, rocking, running, hiding, jumping, climbing or oral behaviors such as sucking, biting, chewing, licking.

Some things EMT personnel can do to help:

• Seek a caregiver. This person will be able to give you quick hints and assistance for communicating and calming the child.

• Simplify communication. Use simple language, gestures and pictures or printed words.

• Minimize sensory input. Provide barriers for excessive auditory and visual input.

Communication Differences

Type	Strategies
Non-verbal	Use gestures and gentle touch, if tolerated. Use visuals. Try pictures first, also words. Keep it simple. Try Yes/No's.
Echolalic	Use visuals: pictures and words. Use gentle touch and gestures to direct attention to important

	information. Keep it simple. Limit your verbal messages.
Perseverates (repeats same thing over and over)	Use gestures and visuals: words and pictures. Use gentle touch as tolerated. Use simple language.
Literal-concrete	Simplify your language. Avoid figurative language. Be specific and clear. Give simple information. Write it down. Use pictures.
Hyperverbal (talks excessively)	Use visuals to help focus. Respond to messages with support and summarize.
Processing Delay	Slow your rate of speech. Simplify language. Wait for response (up to 30 seconds). Use visuals and gestures. Pause frequently in your own language. Write down/make quick cartoons of important information.

Individuals with autism often demonstrate at least some or all of the following characteristics:

• Limited ability to learn incidentally from their environment.

• Limited ability to learn from modeling.

• Limited ability to integrate information that has been learned.

• Limited ability to apply skills that have been learned.

• Differently dispersed attention.

• Difficulty with organizational skills.

• Difficulty with motor planning skills.

• Limited repertoire of exploration skills, especially in over-stimulating situations.

• Limited and unconventional social interaction skills.

• Limited levels of instructional control.

• Unusual responses to sensory stimuli (under responsive, over responsive, limited ability to modulate responses).

• Extremely limited communication skills (verbal and nonverbal).

• Severe movement differences (tics; perseveration; stereotypical behavior; repeated movement patterns; difficulty starting, combining, or switching movement patterns; etc.).

• Unconventional and challenging behavior.

• Apparent limited amount of internal motivation for learning.

• High level of distractibility.

• High activity level.

• High need for predictability and routine.

The simple communication picture system shown above (created with Boardmaker software from Mayer-Johnson, Inc.; see Appendix, page 143) was provided for each emergency medical technician to have with them in the event they encountered someone with autism or other communication challenges.

C. Natural Supports/Peers

One advantage of having students with autism learning in the same environments as typical students is that the classroom peers can become the models and teachers for one another.

Appreciating diversity and understanding individual differences are common themes in contemporary classrooms. There are classrooms that, by nature of how they are set up and operate, innately encourage students to accept and tolerate each other's differences.

Classrooms that discuss what compassion is, and how it's important to at least accept and be kind to others even if you do not like them or understand them, promote tolerance.

Talking to students about the importance of asking questions whenever they feel confused, afraid or hurt can prevent misunderstandings and even bullying. Consider having regular class meetings to facilitate this process around all types of issues, not just those including a student with autism. A listing of materials that may assist creating a classroom of compassion and acceptance can be found in the Appendix under Existing Resources, beginning on page 140.

4. THE MAGIC OF RELATIONSHIP

We began this book with the statement that fear is the enemy of intimacy, and asserted our belief that it is education that can be an antidote to that fear. Coming to know and understand someone better almost always brings with it a growing compassion for who that person is and what it's like for him or her to be in this world. It is through this coming to know others and the resulting development of relationships with them that we can all grow and learn, moving toward families, play groups, classrooms, and communities that are more open and accepting of everyone.

It is not only our belief that this can happen, but also more importantly, our experience. We've chosen a few examples of enlightened relationships to share with you here.

Sibling Compassion

In one of our communities the local public television station sponsored a writing competition in which students in the area middle schools were given the topic, "If you could be anyone for one day, who would you choose and why." Megan Matthews, whose younger brother Mark has autism, had spent a great deal of time trying to learn about the disorder that challenged her brother daily. In expressing her wish to know the experience of his challenges even more intimately, she won with the following essay. Megan was an 11-year-old in the sixth grade when she wrote this essay. The level of understanding and compassion which permeates her writing is an example of what can happen when children understand each other and when their learning environments, both home and school, are safe enough to allow them to be who they naturally are.

My Brother
By Megan Matthews

I know most people would probably want to be someone famous like Michael Jordan or Dominique Moceanu, but not me. I want to be someone very different from the rest of us, my brother.

My brother Mark is very special because he has autism. Autism is a disability that prevents someone from speaking. My brother is nine and is beginning to speak a lot more than he used to.

Autism is a lifelong disability that makes it hard for the person to say what he or she feels. It is also hard on the family because they aren't always able to understand what the autistic person wants and needs. Like normal people, autistic people can be very stubborn at times and wonderful at others.

The reason I chose my brother was because I wanted to know what my brother is thinking and feeling and what he wants. Then maybe I would be able to help other people to know what autism is and how we can help.

I also want to know what it would be like to be trapped inside a body that hears and understands everything but most of the time can't express himself verbally.

Sometimes he can type on a computer to tell us what's wrong and what he wants but not always. I think it'd be exciting to be my brother for a day.

Our Children

Our own children frequently have the opportunity to come to know people with autism through the work that we do. They meet them in our homes, in our offices, as peer playmates in playgroups, and as friends who have become part of our social network and extended family.

Once again, a writing assignment provided the opportunity for reflection about the experience of autism. As a part of a seventh grade English class, one of our children was asked to write a story about someone named Grunt Bearclaws who most people thought was hard and challenging to know. Following is the assignment she completed:

Grunt Bearclaws
By Carissa Shoultz

This story is dedicated to Matthew Nagle, a teenager with autism. Grunt Bearclaws is the kind of person Matthew was. With the help of good teachers and his parents, Matt is more like you and me now.

Nobody really liked him, and it wasn't just because of his name. His name was Grunt Bearclaws. Some people thought he was the way he was because he had some disease. But there's no disease that makes you the way he was. At least, I don't think there is.

At times he would be so mean he'd make people cry. Like the time he got really mad at Joan when she wouldn't listen to what he was saying about his favorite videos. But he had already told her about them three times. When she said she wouldn't listen anymore he got so mad he screamed at the top of his lungs for her to listen to him. She was so upset she cried, then finally decided to listen to him. He told her the same stories two more times and it made him so happy that she let him, that she couldn't help but feel good about him.

Then there was the time where he couldn't get what he wanted from his parents. This time it happened to be a toy. He got so mad he threw a tantrum. He was screaming, yelling, lying on the ground, and kicking. He did this even though he was in the middle of a great big store. His parents then said that if he could control his behavior for a week, they would buy him that toy.

So all that week, Grunt tried his hardest to keep his behavior under control. There would be times where he almost lost it, but found a way to control himself. This was very hard for Grunt, but he tried his best, for he really wanted that toy.

At the end of the week he had made it. His parents took him back to the store to buy the toy he wanted. Grunt was the happiest boy in town, and kept thanking his parents over and over and over. They couldn't help but love the kid.

He played with that toy for three weeks straight. It was all he would look at. It was all he would play with. It was all he would talk about. And if you didn't listen to him tell you about it, or if you wouldn't play with it with him ... you guessed it ... he'd get really mad and scream at you. People tried to be patient, but some just couldn't stand hearing about this toy over and over. As the weeks went on, he found other things to talk about. People were grateful, until he got stuck talking about those things over and over and over and over. But he liked it so much when they listened. This was the way of Grunt Bearclaws, and you couldn't help but love the kid.

Peer Support

One of the ripple effects of our sensitivity trainings in schools is that it allows peers to become natural supports and educators for one another.

Consider the following story: When a first grade student with autism, Sam, was walking to the playground with a group of students from a number of different grade levels, he began engaging in self-stimulatory behavior in the form of flapping his hands. An upper-classman, who was unfamiliar with Sam, started to giggle and point at him. Immediately, several students from Sam's homeroom class came to Sam's defense, telling the older student to "knock it off" and explained that Sam did that when he was excited sometimes. The older student stopped the teasing and ended the interaction by apologizing to Sam.

These classmates clearly understood Sam and were the best "teachers" of this older student, who was lacking in information, because they were Sam's friends. A way of supporting these kinds of natural child-teaching interactions to occur, is to tap into existing structures in the school environment to teach sensitivity and understanding to the classmates of students with autism.

Friendship

Through our work we have been blessed to see real friendships develop and blossom. As you will see from the next piece, David and Grady have been together for much of their school experience. They met while in preschool together, then later began meeting regularly for a playgroup. Their friendship was thus established and continues today as they are entering high school. Following is a journal entry by Grady:

Happy Memories with David

David V. and I have been friends since preschool. Every other Tuesday for the past seven years, we have been playing with his helper, Nan Negri. Here are some of my favorite memories with David ... I remember the sleepover at Nan's house. It was David's first. We watched a movie and went to bed. The next morning we made Mickey Mouse pancakes. David did excellent on his pancake.

Then there was Noah's Ark [a huge water park]. David had been talking about it a month before we were going to leave. When we got there we had a blast. It was fun for Dave and me.

Last but not least, the Peter, Paul and Mary concert. Peter, Paul and Mary were better than I expected. David sang all of "Puff the Magic Dragon"! Now my family has a lot of Peter, Paul and Mary CDs.

I have learned that all people are the same on the inside but might not be impressive on the outside. David is a growing kid just like me and we should treat him like you treat people without disabilities. I've learned a lot from David and I want to thank him a lot and hope that someday all the people will understand that people with disabilities have feelings and that you can upset them every day. And that one day we will treat everybody as if they were your best friend.

Fruits of Sensitivity Training

We regularly conduct trainings in which we teach others how to do these sensitivity presentations in their schools. Following is an email we received from a teacher who went back to her school and did some sensitivity training of her own:

> Just wanted to let you know how our sensitivity training went with the middle school kids. It was wonderful. We actually had tried not to single out the student with Asperger's syndrome, so we discussed disabilities and did some hands-on with the sensory issues. The kids were very receptive and had many questions for us. We gave the presentation five times that day to various classrooms. The most interesting one was the class where the student was. When we asked what a disability was, he piped up and said, "I have Asperger's." It was amazing. He wanted us to teach him more and to teach his classmates about his issues.
>
> Afterwards he stayed with us and his teacher to ask questions about Asperger's. He was confused about some things and needed more input as to why he is like he is. It was wonderful for us and for the teacher to recognize that these challenges are real for him.
>
> That day they started a peer lunch group because we had so many kids volunteer to be involved with the student with special needs!
>
> We have been called into more buildings since then, especially for staff involved with the students on the spectrum. The sensory component hands-on goes really well!
>
> Thanks again for your help and support.

Conclusion

These examples suggest to us the limitless possibilities when children are supported in the creation of tolerant and compassionate living and learning environments. Our hope is that the openness and creativity of the stories above will be as inspirational to the readers as they have been to us.

To nurture the same kind of creativity and openness in your own students, the reader will need to be able to make these activities as much their own as possible. By no means do the authors consider the activities presented here exhaustive. In fact, the number of ideas for sensitivity training is limited only by your creativity. Each of the activities presented in this book can be individualized and adapted for the classmates and the characteristics present in each individual with autism. As you use the activities and create your own, please feel free to send your adaptations and ideas to us for future sharing at the following email address: bobkat@smallbytes.net.

There is a blank form in the Appendix (page 149) for those who might prefer to send their ideas through the traditional mail. Send your activity ideas to this address:

Cambridge Book Review Press
P. O. Box 222
Cambridge, Wisconsin
53523

As a final note, we would like to say that a source of inspiration for us has been the Tribes philosophy and curriculum, as described by Judith Hamilton Johnson in the Preface to Jeanne Gibbs' book, *TRIBES: A New Way of Learning and Being Together*:

> Tribes TLC [Tribes Learning Community] is about honoring each person's wonderful uniqueness. It is about respecting the intelligence of kids, and about giving up the "guru" role we as teachers and administrators often have played rather than becoming facilitators who call forth the gifts of those whom we teach. This process makes a declaration that as a Tribes school, every child is honored, every parent respected and every teacher a facilitator of learning. (Gibbs 1995, 12)

In the spirit of the Tribes philosophy, we hope that this book will add to the declaration of honoring each person's wonderful uniqueness. By teaching classmates and staff to understand and accept individuals with autism, the general climate of tolerance and acceptance spreads. It is our hope that this climate permeates every crevice of our schools and our hearts.

APPENDIX

I. References

American Psychiatric Association. 2000. *Diagnostic and Statistical Manual of Mental Disorders*. 4th ed. Washington, D. C.: American Psychiatric Publishing, Inc.

Barron, J., and S. Barron. 1992. *There's a Boy in Here*. New York: Simon & Schuster.

Blackman, L. 1999. *Lucy's Story: Autism and Other Adventures*. Brisbane, Australia: Book in Hand.

Cesaroni, L. 1990. Exploring the experience through first-hand accounts from high-functioning individuals with autism. University of Toronto. Unpublished.

Cesaroni, L. 1991. Exploring the experience of autism through first-hand accounts. *Journal of Autism and Developmental Disorders* 21: 303-313.

Bemporad, J. R. 1979. Adult recollections of a formerly autistic child. *Journal of Autism and Developmental Disorders* 9 (2): 179-197.

Donnellan, A. M. 1984. The criterion of the least dangerous assumption. *Behavior Disorders* 9: 141-150.

Donnellan, A. M., and M. R. Leary. 1995. *Movement Differences and Diversity in Autism/Mental Retardation*. Madison, WI: DRI Press.

Garrity, C., K. Jens, W. Porter, N. Sager, and C. Short-Camilli. 1996. *Bully Proofing Your School: A comprehensive approach for elementary schools*. Longmont, CO: Sopris West.

Gibbs, J. 1995. *TRIBES: A new way of learning and being together*. Sausalito, CA: Center Source Systems.

Gillingham, G. 1995. *Autism: Handle with care*. Arlington, TX: Future Horizons.

Gillingham, G., and S. McClennen. 2003. *Sharing Our Wisdom: A collection of presentations by people within the autism spectrum*. Edmonton, Alberta: Tacit Publishing.

Grandin, T. 1983. Letters to the editor. "Coping strategies." *Journal of Autism and Developmental Disorders* 13: 217-221.

Grandin, T. 1984. My experiences as an autistic child. *Journal of Orthomolecular Psychiatry* 13: 144-174.

Grandin, T. 1988. Teaching tips from a recovered autistic. *Focus on Autistic Behaviour* 3: 1-8.

Grandin, T., and M. Scariano. 1986. *Emergence: Labeled autistic.* Urbana, IL: Arena Press.

Gray, C. 2002. *The Sixth Sense II.* Arlington, TX: Future Horizons.

Groden, J., and P. LeVasseur. 1995. Cognitive picture rehearsal: A system to teach self-control. In *Teaching Children with Autism: Strategies to enhance communication and socialization,* ed. K. A. Quill, 287-307. New York: Delmar Publishers.

Groden, J., J. Cautela, and G. Groden, producer. *Breaking the Barriers I: Relaxation techniques for people with special needs.* Champaign, IL: Research Press, 1989. Videotape and guide.

Hale, M., and C. Hale. 1999. *I Had No Means to Shout!* Bloomington, IN: 1st Books.

Hodgdon, L. 1995. *Visual Strategies for Improving Communication.* Troy, MI: QuirkRoberts Publishing.

Hurlburt, R. T., F. Happe, and U. Frith. 1994. Sampling the form of innerexperience in three adults with Asperger's Syndrome. *Psychological Medicine* 24: 385-395.

Kurtz, A. 1995. Systems shifts and shutdowns: Notes from Donna Williams' keynote. *Facilitated Communication in Maine, An Update* 4 (2).

Lawson, W. 1998. *Life Behind Glass.* London: Jessica Kingsley Publishers.

McKean, T. 1994. *Soon Will Come the Light.* Arlington, TX: Future Horizons.

Morgenstern, C. 1991. In *The Art of the Possible: A comprehensive approach to understanding the way people think, learn & communicate,* D. Markova. Berkeley, CA: Conari Press.

Mukhopadhyay, T. R. 2000. *Beyond the Silence.* London: National Autistic Society.

Patterson, J. 2002. Movement differences: Data collected from first-hand accounts of autism. University of San Diego. Unpublished.

Pawlisch, J. S. 1998. *Pupil Records of Children with Exceptional Educations Needs.* Bulletin No. 98.02. Wisconsin Department of

Public Instruction: Information Update.

Prizant, B., and J. Duchan. 1981. The functions of immediate echolalia in autistic children. *Journal of Speech and Hearing Disorders* 46 (3): 241-249.

Prizant, B. 1983. Echolalia in autism: Assessment and intervention. *Seminars in Speech and Language* 4: 63-67.

Strandt-Conroy, K. 1999. Exploring movement differences in autism through first-hand accounts. Dissertation, University of Wisconsin-Madison.

Williams, D. 1992. *Nobody Nowhere*. New York: Times Books.

Williams, D. 1994. *Somebody Somewhere*. New York: Times Books.

Williams, D. 1996. *Like Color to the Blind*. New York: Times Books.

Williams, D. 1996. *Autism: An inside-out approach*. London: Jessica Kingsley Publishers.

Williams, D. 1998. *Autism and Sensing: The unlost instinct*. London: Jessica Kingsley Publishers.

Williams, M., and S. Shellenberger. 1994. *How Does Your Engine Run?: A leader's guide to the alert program for self-regulation*. Albuquerque, NM: TherapyWorks, Inc.

Wing, Lorna. 1993. *Autistic Continuum Disorders, 2nd ed*. National Autistic Society.

II. Existing Resources

A. Suggested Books to Use with Sensitivity Activities

Bailey, Carolyn Sherwin. [1978] 1988. *The Little Rabbit Who Wanted Red Wings*. Reprint, New York: Grosset & Dunlap.

Cairo, Shelley. 1985. *Our Brother Has Down's Syndrome*. Toronto: Annick Press.

Cannon, Janell. 1993. *Stellaluna*. New York: Harcourt.

Carle, Eric. [1975] 1988. *The Mixed-Up Chameleon*. Reprint, New York: HarperTrophy.

Carlson, Nancy L. 1990. *I Like Me!* New York: Penguin USA.

Clements, Andrew. [1988] 1997. *Big Al*. Reprint, New York: Simon & Schuster.

Cowen-Fletcher, Jane. [1993] 1999. *Mama Zooms*. Reprint, New York: Scholastic.

Dwyer, Kathleen M. 1991. *What Do You Mean I Have a Learning Disability?* New York: Walker & Co.

Faulkner, Keith. 1991. *Boastful Bullfrog*. Stamford, CT: Longmeadow Press.

Faulkner, Keith. 1990. *Elephant and the Rainbow*. Stamford, CT: Longmeadow Press.

Fleming, Virginia. [1993] 1997. *Be Good to Eddie Lee*. Reprint, New York: Penguin USA.

Gillingham, G., and S. McClennen. 2003. *Sharing Our Wisdom: A collection of presentations by people within the autism spectrum*. Edmonton, Alberta: Tacit Publishing.

Grandin, T., and M. Scariano. 1986. *Emergence: Labeled autistic*. Urbana, IL: Arena Press.

Hallinan, P.K. [1997] 2002. *That's What a Friend Is*. Reprint, Nashville: Ideal Publications.

Heinrichs, Rebekah. 2003. *Perfect Targets: Asperger syndrome and bullying—Practical solutions for surviving the social world*. Shawnee Mission, KS: Autism Asperger Publishing Co.

Henkes, Kevin. 1996. *Chrysanthemum*. New York: HarperTrophy.

Howe, James. 1987. *I Wish I Were a Butterfly*. San Diego: Gulliver Books/Harcourt.

Jackson, Luke. 2002. *Freaks, Geeks & Asperger Syndrome: A user guide to adolescence*. New York: Routledge.

Jampolsky, Gerald G., and Diane V. Cirincione. 1991. *Me First and the Gimme Gimmes*. Deerfield Beach, FL: Health Communications, Inc.

Janover, Caroline. 1988. *Josh: A Boy with Dyslexia*. Burlington, VT: Waterfront Books.

Lester, Helen. 1990. *Tacky the Penguin*. Boston: Houghton Mifflin.

Mayer, Mercer. 1998. *Just a Little Different*. New York: Golden Books.

McPhail, David. [1993] 1998. *Santa's Book of Names*. Reprint, New York: Little, Brown.

Osofsky, Audrey. 1994. *My Buddy*. New York: Henry Holt.

Pfister, Marcus. 1992. *The Rainbow Fish*. New York: North-South Books.

Roby, Cynthia. 1994. *When Learning is Tough: Kids talk about learning disabilities*. Morton Grove, IL: Albert Whitman.

Shles, Larry. 1989. *Do I Have To Go To School Today?* Carson, CA: Jalmar Press.

Steiner, Claude. [1977] 1985. *The Original Warm Fuzzy Tale*. Reprint, Carson, CA: Jalmar Press.

Suess, Dr. 1961. *The Sneetches and Other Stories*. New York: Random House.

Wildsmith, Brian. 1972. *The Owl and the Woodpecker*. New York: Franklin Watts.

Wright, Betty Ren. 1981. *My Sister Is Different*. Crystal Lake, IL: Raintree.

Yashima, Taro. [1955] 1976. *Crow Boy*. Reprint, New York: Penguin USA.

B. Sensitivity/Awareness Books for Children

Amenta III, Charles A. 1992. *Russell is Extra Special: A book about autism for children*. New York: Magination Press.

Band, Eve B., and Emily Hecht. 2001. *Autism through a Sister's Eyes*. Arlington, TX: Future Horizons.

Bishop, Beverly. 2003. *My Friend with Autism: A coloring book for peers and siblings*. Arlington, TX: Future Horizons.

Bleach, Fiona. 2002. *Everybody is Different: A book for young people who have brothers or sisters with autism*. Shawnee Mission, KS: Autism Asperger Publishing Co.

Edwards, Becky, and David Armitage. 1999. *My Brother Sammy*. Brookfield, CT: Millbrook Press.

Emigh, Karen. 2003. *Who Took My Shoe?* Arlington, TX: Future Horizons.

Espin, Roz. 2003. *Amazingly ... Alphie! Understanding and accepting different ways of being*. Shawnee Mission, KS: Autism Asperger Publishing Co.

Gagnon, Elisa, and Brenda Smith Myles. 1999. *This is Asperger Syndrome*. Shawnee Mission, KS: Autism Asperger Publishing Co.

Kahn, Robert. 2001. *Too Safe for Strangers*. Arlington, TX: Future Horizons.

Kahn, Robert. 2001. *Too Smart for Bullies*. Arlington, TX: Future Horizons.

Katz, Illana, and Edward Ritvo. 1993. *Joey and Sam: A heartwarming storybook about autism, a family, and a brother's love*. Northridge, CA: Real Life Story Books.

Lears, Laurie. [1998] 2003. *Ian's Walk: A story about autism*. Reprint, Morton Grove, IL: Albert Whitman.

Maguire, Arlene. 2000. *Special People, Special Ways*. Arlington, TX: Future Horizons.

Messner, Abby Ward. 1996. *Captain Tommy*. Arlington, TX: Future Horizons.

Mitchell, Lori. 1999. *Different Just Like Me*. Watertown, MA: Charlesbridge Publishing.

Murrell, Diane. 2001. *Tobin Learns to Make Friends*. Arlington, TX: Future Horizons.

Peralta, Sarah. 2002. *All About My Brother*. Shawnee Mission, KS: Autism Asperger Publishing Co.

Sprecher, John. 1997. *Jeffrey and the Despondent Dragon*. Baltimore: Special Kids Company.

Thompson, Mary. 1996. *Andy and His Yellow Frisbee*. Bethesda: Woodbine House.

Shore, Stephen. 2003. *Beyond the Wall: Personal experiences with autism and asperger syndrome*. 2nd ed. Shawnee Mission, KS: Autism Asperger Publishing Co.

Simmons, Karen. 1996. *Little Rainman*. Arlington, TX: Future Horizons.

Watson, Esther. 1996. *Talking to Angels*. New York: Harcourt.

C. Videos, Software, DVDs & CDs

A is for Autism. 1992. Directed by Tim Webb. 11 min. UK: Channel 4. Videocassette. (Available online from www.films.com. Phone: 800-257-5126. Email: custserv@films.com.)

Boardmaker [Computer software]. 2000. Solana Beach, CA: Mayer-Johnson, Inc. (Available online from www.mayer-johnson.com. Phone: 800-588-4548. Email: mayerj@mayer-johnson.com.)

Don't Laugh at Me. 2000. New York: Operation Respect. Multi-media. (Available online from the DLAM website, www.dontlaugh.org.)

Dr. Temple Grandin. 2003. 120 min. Arlington, TX: Future Horizons. DVD. (Contains four 30-minute programs originally released in 1999 on videocassette: *Careers—Opportunity for Growth*; *Medications—Fact and Fiction*; *Sensory Challenges and Answers*; *Visual Thinking of a Person with Autism*. Available online from www.futurehorizons-autism.com.)

Souls: Beneath and beyond autism. 2003. Sharon Rosenbloom and Thomas Balsamo. Barrington, IL: Books that Touch. DVD.

Straight Talk About Autism with Parents and Kids. 2002. 80 min. Verona, WI: Attainment Company, Inc. DVD. (Contains two 40-minute programs originally released in 1999 on videocassette:

Straight Talk About Autism with Parents and Kids: Childhood issues; *Straight Talk About Autism with Parents and Kids: Adolescent issues.* Available online from www.attainmentcompany.com.)

Tunes for Knowing and Growing. 1997. Jeanne Lyons. Audio cassette/CD. (Available from Jeanne Lyons, P. O. Box 72857, Marietta, GA 30007.)

III. Autism: Basic Facts

• Autism was first named by Leo Kanner in 1943.

• Autism affects children from all ethnic and socio-economic backgrounds.

• Autism occurs at a rate of approximately 20 to 25 per 10,000 births. This represents the full spectrum.

• Autism affects boys more frequently than girls (4:1).

• Autism is a neurological disorder.

• Autism has a variety of biological causes: e.g.,
  —genetic factors
  —viral infections
  —birth or pregnancy complications
  —other

• These biological causes are not found in every child with autism. There remain unknown biological causes.

• Autism appears in the first three years of life.

• Autism can occur in combination with other disabilities.

• Autism occurs on a continuum from mild to severe.

IV. Autism: Learning Characteristics

Learners who have autism often demonstrate at least some or all of the following characteristics:

• Limited ability to learn incidentally from their environment.

• Limited ability to learn from modeling.

• Limited ability to integrate information that has been learned.

• Limited ability to apply skills that have been learned.

• Limited ability to generalize skill development.

• Differently dispersed attention.

• Difficulty with organizational skills.

• Difficulty with motor planning skills.

• Limited repertoire of exploration skills, especially in overstimulating situations.

• Limited and unconventional social interaction skills.

• Limited levels of instructional control.

• Unusual responses to sensory stimuli (under responsive, over responsive, limited ability to modulate responses).

• Extremely limited communication skills (verbal and nonverbal).

- Severe movement differences (tics; perseveration; stereotypical behavior; repeated movement patterns; difficulty starting, combining, or switching movement patterns; etc.).

- Unconventional and challenging behavior.

- Apparent limited amount of internal motivation for learning.

- High level of distractibility.

- High activity level.

- High need for predictability and routine.

With systematic and direct instruction learners are able to significantly alter the difficulties they experience in learning and in functioning. Learning strategies are developed and coping mechanisms are taught such that individuals begin to learn from and with their same-aged peers.

V. Student Survey Form

1. You have had the opportunity to be with (student's name) for about (amount of time). What questions do you have about him and/or his abilities? What are you curious about? What would you like to know about (student's name) and/or autism?

2. How do other kids treat (student's name) in the cafeteria, hallway classroom, bus, etc.? Are they helpful, nice, kind, mean? Do some people just ignore him? Do people seem afraid of him?

3. What do you think YOU can do to help (student's name) feel more comfortable and fit in more for the amount of time he is in your class? (Examples: greet him daily, invite him to join your group, invite him to try to remain with the activity, offer to photocopy your notes for him to study from, etc.)

VI. Activities Form

Activity:

Description:

You will need:

Major points to make:

√

√

√

VII. Contact Information for Matthew Ward

Matthew Ward
c/o Nancy Alar
3802 Gala Way
Cottage Grove, WI
53527

Email: talar@tds.net

Phone: 608-222-4378

ACKNOWLEDGMENTS

This book was possible because of the lessons offered to us by the many individuals on the autism spectrum who grace our lives with their presence. In this often challenging and confusing field they have helped to keep us grounded and have been our finest teachers. We are deeply grateful to all of you for sharing your experiences, for teaching us so well, and for the richness you bring to our lives. We would also like to thank the friends and colleagues who generously contributed their ideas and/or feedback to our writing.

People gave to this project in varied fashions. Thank you to the following for contributing directly to our book: Matt Ward, Dylan Shroud, Mark Matthews, Megan Matthews, Carissa Shoultz, Grady Brown, Heidi Martel, Sarah Pedersen, Sharon Smith, and Gail Stark.

Other people provided inspiration and ideas which we adapted as activities in this book. Thank you to: Michael Shoultz, Barb Renfro, Patty Mader-Ebert, Janet Madners, Deborah Kowalkowski-Funk, Jane Webfer, and Susan Vaughan Kratz.

And then there were our generous associates, cohorts, and friends who gave of their precious time to review our work and give their very useful feedback: Jenny Potanos, Mary Gracyzk-McMullen, Donna Rosinski, Sally Young, and John Lehman. Your willingness to give of yourselves to this project warms our hearts and allows this book to reflect the positive effect of collaboration that we think is essential in all of our work and, in fact, our lives.

There were several people who went above and beyond the call of collegial support and offered amazing skills, words, and insight for us. The first of those is Temple Grandin, who assisted us in further understanding the perspective of autism by the observations and comments she supplied as a peer reviewer of our book. Temple, you are a treasure to us and to this field. The second is our brilliant mentor and friend, Anne M. Donnellan, who read our book under the wire of the deadline of her son's wedding plans and supplied us with invaluable ideas as well as the skills and the willingness of her able graduate student, Jodi Patterson. Anne and Jodi, we will never be able to appropriately thank you for your incredible work on our behalf related to this book.

And, of course, we thank our beloved and supportive families. Nathan, Carissa and Augie ... from your beginnings you inspired us to include you in the lives of our friends on the spectrum. Through your openness of heart and willingness to play, you validated for us that ALL children can learn from one another and can come to love one another ... not just in spite of differences, but because of them.

Michael and Todd, your connection to one another has provided a cohesion in our families that has enhanced our creative process and our lives.

Ben and Bob, you have been ideal partners, providing inspiration, love and support to this project and our lives. Thank you for contributing your skills and talents to this book. We couldn't have completed it without you.

ABOUT THE AUTHORS

Kate McGinnity

Kate is an experienced classroom teacher and trainer, and a nationally recognized consultant in the field of autism. She has over twenty years' experience working with individuals with autism and their families. During her tenure as a teacher, she was recognized as the Wisconsin Teacher of the Year and the National Teacher of the Year by the Autism Society of America. Together with her husband, Kate had the honor of foster parenting an adolescent on the autism spectrum for two and a half years. She is currently in private practice, providing training and consultation to professionals and parents, as well as counseling to individuals on the autism spectrum.

Nan Negri

Nan has over thirty years' experience as a teacher and trainer, and as a consultant in the field of autism. She has written autism-related articles and chapters and has co-authored a book on non-aversive behavior management strategies. As a member of the National Personnel Training Team, Nan has provided a trainer of trainers model to programming for individuals with autism. Currently, Nan is in private practice, providing consultation and training to school districts in several states, consultation to families, and direct treatment and yoga to individuals on the spectrum. She believes relationship and fun are the keys to learning for all of us.